Boomers on the Loose™ In Portland

Every Retiree's Guide to Staying Active in Portland

Janet Farr

Boomers on the Loose™ LLC
Hillsboro, Oregon

Copyright 2017 Janet A. Farr. All rights reserved.

No part of this book may be reproduced in any form without written permission from the author.

Photographs by the author unless otherwise noted.

Editing by Bill Cowles

Cover design by Lyn Birmingham

Cover art © 2017 by Joshua Cleland (JoshCleland.com)

The inclusion of any place of business in this book should not be taken as an endorsement by the author or publisher. Facts stated in this book are to the best of the author's knowledge true. Website URLs, maps, business operations and other specifics are subject to change without notice.

Wherever possible, the author has obtained the permission to photograph persons whose likenesses are included in this book. The inclusion of any person's likeness in this book should not be taken as an endorsement of the book, the author, or any matters pertaining to this publication.

Users of this book expressly agree that their use is at their sole risk.

The intent of this book is to provide ideas as to leisure activities available to retirees in and around Portland. A large portion of the information included is based on information publicly published on the Internet and was believed to be accurate approximately 30 days prior to publishing.

IBSN: 978-0-9989871-0-1

Library of Congress Control Number: 2017909244

Table of Contents

INTRODUCTION

It's a great time to be a Baby Boomer. Every day, Boomers are discovering that "retirement" is simply an avenue toward "re-inventment!" Life isn't winding down for Boomers – it's amping up! And that's why this book is chock full of Boomer resources – to make it easy for you to find exactly what you want to do and be in this exciting new life chapter.

Research shows that Boomers want to live with purpose and fulfillment. They want to be active and productive. They want to dig in the dirt, plant and harvest community gardens, restore wetlands and wildlife habitat. They like to guide groups around nature centers, art galleries and museums. Many serve on public committees. Others teach kids to read, play music, dance, garden or create art. They learn music, lead hikes, paddle dragon boats, walk goats at the zoo, count birds and clean up parks. Boomers learn new skills and start businesses. They study the world, meet new people, volunteer, improve our communities and lots more.

We hope you're getting the idea that Boomer status can be pretty darn exciting!

We also realize that this phase can be intimidating – "What do I do now?" That's why we created *Boomers on the Loose™ in Portland* – to take the anxiety out of your quest for "what's next?" In this book, you'll be able to explore relevant and current options for meaningful leisure pursuits in hundreds of interest areas. All in one place.

You'll learn more about how to pursue your interests or develop new ones in retirement. Just start in your interest area – such as animal lovers, gardening, hiking and walking, volunteering, learning, or caring for the environment, for example. Then browse through all of the options for Portland area activities, events, clubs, diversions, volunteer activities and relevant websites.

How We Organized Boomers on The Loose™ In Portland

Discovering that we were trying to make sense of ever-changing information, we divided *Boomers on the Loose™ in Portland* into two major parts:

INTEREST SECTION. Here you can identify and read about leisure retirement activities that appeal to you. These first 20 chapters direct you to broad interest categories, for example, Gardening. Each topic is further divided into another layer of interests, introducing ideas and options for enthusiasts.

RESOURCE APPENDICES. View tons of descriptive lists of related places, organizations, clubs, activities and events here in Portland. Just follow our resource listings of specific organizations, clubs and places to zero in on specific websites to visit.

You'll also notice that the activities included are those that put attention on existing, mostly inexpensive or free activities in our area. We help you find things to do in places like community colleges, parks and recreation organizations, senior and community centers, non-profits, government agencies, outdoor organizations and open-to-everyone clubs and groups.

Our research started with an extensive search of the most popular activities Boomers currently enjoy in retirement and researched hundreds of organizations.

Boomers on the Loose™ in Portland is intended to evolve – with little pre-conceived notion of what it should look like. The process and our readers will lead us to what it will become, realizing that it will change as our landscape changes.

So get ready to do something big, Boomers. Use our resources to zero in on your passion, then check back here and on our website, BoomersontheLoose.com often to see what's new on the Boomer landscape!

Have fun out there – Portland awaits...!

CHAPTER 1: ANIMAL LOVER OPPORTUNITIES

Every day, Portland area Boomers pour their love for animals into many channels of volunteer work to improve the lives of rescue cats, dogs, horses and other animals.

- They care for animals that have been abused and abandoned.

- They feed, walk, and work with animals at the zoo.

- They team up with therapy animals.

- If animals occupy your special heart place, get involved in animal-related volunteer work. You'll discover interesting, fulfilling and out-of-the ordinary opportunities.

Animal Rescue and Adoption

If your heart goes out to homeless, sick, abandoned or abused animals, volunteering in animal rescue and adoption may be a rewarding activity for you. All types of animal shelters exist in the Portland area and rely on volunteers to fulfill a wide variety of shelter caregiving jobs. Small animal shelters nearly always need volunteers to help out with the following:

- Feeding animals
- Socializing animals
- Fostering and adoption
- Veterinarian care

- Transporting pets
- Working outreach events
- Office and clerical work
- Photography, graphic arts

Horse rescue operations care for at-risk horses that have been abandoned, abused, neglected, lost, or simply unwanted. They care for them until permanent homes can be found. Some operations combine horse rescue with equine-assisted therapy. Horse rescue activities involve feeding, grooming, cleaning stalls, fundraising, helping with special events, doing clerical work, and other jobs.

See *APPENDIX A: ANIMAL RESCUE AND ADOPTION* on page 75 for a list of animal rescue organizations and their volunteer needs.

Animal-assisted Therapy Programs

People-animal teams seek to improve the lives of others. They brighten the days of those they visit in hospitals, hospice, nursing homes, mental institutions, and other places. Their visits calm the emotionally challenged, give confidence to the disabled and connect to those with special needs. They bring smiles to children a hospital, the elderly in nursing homes, and patients and families in hospice, nursing homes and treatment centers. In libraries, children improve reading skills by reading to special dogs, by nature, non-judgmental listeners.

Special training is required to certify people pet teams for animal-assisted therapy visits.

In the Portland Area Canine Therapy Teams (PACTT) program, people team up with a highly-trained career change dog adopted from Guide Dogs for the Blind. An extensive training and assessment program is offered through DoveLewis Animal Assisted Therapy & Education. The Animal-Assisted Therapy Training Program offered by Oregon Humane Society prepares individuals and their animals to become registered AAT teams with the national organization Pet Partners.

Another animal-assisted therapy program is The Little Dog Laughed. Trained volunteer dog/handler pairs help teach relationship and problem-solving skills to at-risk youth through classes in positive dog training.

Project POOCH, Inc., re-homes shelter dogs, teaching youth in corrections to care for and train shelter dogs for adoption to help them develop personal and vocational skills

Equine-assisted Therapy Programs

If you enjoy working with horses and want to make a difference in lives of people, consider volunteering in an equine-assisted therapy program. Health professionals conduct animal-assisted programs as part of an individual therapy program. In equine-assisted therapy, individuals receive hands-on training in horsemanship to address various disorders and disabilities.

Depending upon your interest, experience and skills, you can participate in therapy sessions, side walk (on either side of horse and rider), or help feed, groom, brush, or clean horse stalls. You can get involved in clerical and fundraising activities, or help at special events. You'll get training in the area of your interest.

Therapy Riding Centers

- BEAT Riding Center. Teaches horsemanship to physically, mentally and emotionally challenged individuals. Banks.

- Chehalem Mountain Therapy Riding Center. Interactions with horses to improve the lives of persons with special needs. Camps.

- Forward Stride. Therapy and veterans' programs. Beaverton.

- Happy Trails Riding Center. Therapeutic riding center for children and adults with disabilities and special needs. Oregon City.

- Horses of Hope. An Equine Therapy experience. Improves lives of people with physical, emotional, and behavioral challenges through equine assisted programs. Turner.

CHAPTER 2: ARTS & CULTURE

The arts and culture scene reflects Portland – rich, vibrant, and diverse. And, of course, it's edgy and off-the-grid and experimental. Boomers find their next phase an exciting time to get immersed in thriving art and culture scenes.

For all with cultural involvement interests, Portland is blessed with world class fine arts and performing arts, and offers a rich array of places for seniors to serve as volunteers. The area offers a booming local arts, theater, music and film scene. Museums satisfy every taste. You can attend, produce or participate in shows and exhibits. You can take arts and culture to those off-stage. You can discover many ways to enrich your life and give back.

Your choices are endless because Portland overflows with places to get involved with your favorite cultural activity ...

- Usher theater and music patrons at Portland'5 Centers for the Arts
- Change sets in Vancouver's delightfully home-grown and ambitious Magenta Theater
- Help put on a festival
- Tell your story on stage
- Help low-income youth express themselves in art, photography or music

Literary Arts

Two popular interests that Boomers enjoy more in retirement are reading and writing. We love stories and want to discover others' and express our own.

That shouldn't surprise us because we enjoy more leisure time. We want to experience new lands, worlds and even galaxies through books. We want to better understand our changing, complex world, current events, our communities and the human journey.

And thanks to ever-growing technology, new books and authors in every genre stream to us. We can instantly order, borrow and download books on any subject, direct from bookstores and libraries to our computers or readers.

On the flip side, many Boomers are fulfilling their dreams to write. Whether crafting a memoir or coming of age story, a sci-fi, romance, fantasy or time travel, Boomers are taking up their pens and keyboards to release their creativity, imagination and desire to learn and grow.

Boomer Readers

In addition to friends, library mailings, and book reviews, Boomer readers have access to other fun connections with books in Portland. Some of the most common come through book clubs, reader events at libraries, author readings and book festivals.

Book clubs are small reader groups who select, read and discuss books. Book clubs are often formed around a genre or common interest. You'll find book clubs of every imaginable type in libraries, senior and community centers, faith-based organizations, bookstores, community organizations and many other gathering places.

Boomers also can choose from a wide selection of book club Meetups throughout the area.

Bookstores, libraries, and several literary organizations sponsor events such as readings, discussion groups and book festivals to bring readers, books and authors together. The best-known are:

- 45NW Book Festival. A free outdoor book fair representing all genres held annually in July.

- Wordstock. A Festival of readers and authors featuring author speakers, workshops and a book fair. Held annually in November. Sponsored by Literary Arts.

See *APPENDIX B, Literary Arts* on page 78 for a list of organizations that sponsor book festivals, readings and other resources to help Portland readers discover their next great read.

Boomer Writers and Authors

If writing is a bucket list item for you, Portland is a place to realize your dream. We're surrounded by a prolific and growing community of authors, poets, bloggers, screenwriters, playwrights and others who encourage and celebrate the written words of others. From beginners to published authors, fiction and non-fiction, across disparate genres and all forms of writing, like-minded people are eager to support and celebrate your success.

No matter where your writing career is aimed, there are energetic organizations to help you learn, write, get feedback, publish and socialize. There is a wide assortment of Writing Meetups throughout the area that offer more choices for authors, writers, bloggers and poets of all interests and abilities.

See *APPENDIX B, Literary Arts* on page 79 for a list of organizations where you can attend writing workshops, participate in critique groups, attend readings, hear speakers and share your knowledge and expertise.

Other places where aspiring and experienced writers can practice and learn their craft include several area community colleges and parks and recreation programs. Writing classes cover fiction, non-fiction, memoir, poetry, short story, business and technical writing, and many other topics.

See *APPENDIX B, Literary Arts Resources* on page 80 for a list of community education and parks and recreation programs that offer writing classes.

Music Arts

For many Boomers, love of music plays some role in their leisure time choices. Portland's musical offerings are as diverse as the city itself – Bluegrass, folk, Indie rock, jazz, classical, pop and more. The music scene offers a tremendous variety of ways to be involved, whether you play an instrument, want to help young musicians or just plain appreciate music.

Some ways Boomers express their love of music include:

- Performing in local bands or orchestras.
- Attending live concerts.
- Working concerts behind the scenes.
- Learning or expanding their own music knowledge and skills.
- Teaching others.
- Performing in hospitals, nursing homes, senior facilities.

Volunteering in Music

Many Boomers broaden their enjoyment of music by volunteering with organizations that perform, teach and reach out to the music-loving community.

Concerts in large venues such as the Portland Symphony Orchestra rely on volunteers assigned through the venue such as Portland'5. In some cases, a "Friends-of…" group, such as the Friends of the Vancouver Symphony Orchestra, fill the volunteer roles. Volunteering information is generally available on each organization's website, though sometimes you may have to creatively dig for it.

Similarly, if you enjoy being immersed in the festival scene, volunteers work in all aspects of stage set-up and take-down, electronics, assisting performers, serving refreshments and activities unique to the concert.

Several youth music organizations rely on volunteers to help make music accessible to everyone. Volunteers help teach and mentor, maintain instruments, set up and host events, fundraising and office activities.

In addition to working directly with performing artists, volunteer benefits may include concert passes and patron and recognition events. Music organizations need volunteers in tasks such as office data entry and filing, answering the phone, fundraising, marketing, writing, graphic design, ushering, ticket taking and serving refreshments. Some take music to their audiences and will put you to work in outreach programs.

See *APPENDIX B, Music Arts Organizations* on page 80 for lists of music organizations and other resources including youth music volunteering.

Performing Arts – Theatre, Dance, Festivals

Boomers love theater. Do you secretly yearn to get on stage? Or volunteer behind the scenes? What resonates with you? Where can you get involved? An ever-changing theater landscape offers limitless opportunities to engage in all aspects of theater.

Portland beckons theater-lovers with rich, vibrant, opportunities for every interest and budget. Large, established venues anchor the theatrical panorama, enriched with a delightful, diverse mixture of quality regional and local productions. You can choose innovative and experimental, ethnic and social statement, and ambitious blends with original music and visual arts media.

From new and original to classical, to new twists on timeless favorites, to the innovative and extremely physical, it's on stage here. Passionate homegrown PDX troupes even perform on converted warehouse stages. Choose from mime, clowns, puppets and street theater, to popular summer outdoor stages.

Youth theater, classes and outreach bring theater to all communities.

See *APPENDIX B, Performing Arts Companies and Venues* on page 85 for a list of all types of theater groups and places in and around Portland.

But for Boomers, the actual performance by actors, directors and musicians is the tip of the iceberg in theater.

Being on Stage: Acting and Storytelling

Want to lose the timid and get on stage? Haven't acted since junior high? You're in the right place. Do a little homework first, though, because theaters have different needs and prerequisites for performers. Large and medium-sized professional theaters generally cast and hire equity and non-equity actors. Smaller and independent theaters may stage productions with a volunteer (unpaid) cast. Some train you in advance. Others give you on-the-set training.

Smaller community theaters are good starting places because of their all-volunteer cast and crew. For example, at the Magenta Theatre in downtown Vancouver, you can audition to act, understudy someone, or work hands-on behind the scenes. Or learn about acting or improv. Tasks such as building and taking down sets, changing scenes, sewing costumes, running the lights and helping on show nights is a fun way to learn theater ins and outs.

Storytelling is another great way to get in front of an audience. Storytellers share vivid personal stories on stage, believing that to be human is to have a story to share. Special workshops help storytellers learn how to develop and present stories to live audiences. Interested? Attend a show. Story theater groups include:

- Portland Storytellers Guild. Storytellers share stories monthly, teach storytelling skills to ordinary people, and hold free "story" swaps to introduce the craft.

- Portland Story Theatre. Gives voice to the true stories of ordinary people through workshops and puts them in front of audience.

- Back Fence PDX. Offers performances and storytelling and writing classes.

Behind the Scenes

Off-stage roles are filled with people like you who make it happen, and theater volunteering attracts volunteers for many reasons. The joy of being creatively involved in making plays happen. Using a special skill or interest such as construction, costuming, music, organizing or meeting the public. Or the simple desire to experience it up close.

Volunteers greet and usher. They design, build and change sets, sew costumes, apply makeup. Manage lighting, sound and music. Work in the back office selling tickets, creating flyers, maintaining lists and doing mailings. Design brochures, take photos. Sell refreshments and gifts. Meet the public at special events and outreach activities. Or plan those activities.

See *APPENDIX B, Performing Arts Theatre Scene* on page 83 for descriptions of the types of theater you can choose from to participate in, attend or work behind the scenes.

Dance

Portland's dance scene ranges from ballet concerts to contemporary work by local companies and collaborations with other art forms. Many take their innovations to local communities. Dance companies in greater Portland include:

- Oregon Ballet Theatre. Oregon's largest professional ballet company rooted in traditions of classical ballet. Ballet school. Volunteers assist with office and at performances.

- Metro Dancers. Portland Metro Arts. Dance productions, repertory concerts and showcases and major ballet by pre-and professional dancers. Volunteers help with fundraising, office work, classes, performances, facilities and grounds.

- Northwest Dance Theatre. Pre-professional dance performances, community outreach and educational programs.

- Polaris Dance Theatre. Contemporary dance company and dance center for youth and classes. Volunteers usher, setup/strike at productions, help with costumes, tables and committees.

- White Bird. Brings Portland-based, as well as regional, national, and international dance companies to Portland. Collaborates with area arts organizations. Community outreach. Volunteers usher, help with office, poster distribution, loading in/out shows, special events.

Performing Arts Festivals

Annual festivals are another way to experience the area's new, emerging and fringe theater, dance and other performances. Among them:

- Fertile Ground. Two weeks focused on new work in the arts including staged readings developing woks and myriad of other arts events from local artists, performers and resident theater companies. Portland Theatre Alliance. January.

- JAW. Portland Center Stage. A playwright's festival of staged readings of new scripts and performances from Portland theaters and arts ensembles. July.

- Time-Based Art Festival (TBA). Portland Institute for Contemporary Art. Features fresh new wave of art in real time from performing and visual artists hailing from all over the world. Installations and live performances fill out area theaters, temporary galleries and unexpected public spaces. Volunteers help in construction, administration, exhibitions. September.

Visual Arts: Art, Photography, Film

Does your interest gravitate to some aspect of Portland's energetic and dynamic visual art scene? If so, you'll discover dozens of places to interact with your favorite art form by learning, volunteering or participating in art-full communities of artists, film-makers and photographers.

You can attend exhibits ranging from the highly-regarded collections at the Portland Art Museum, to local and regional shows at community art centers, to collections throughout public and private venues.

You're surrounded by art in all media embedded throughout community landscapes and within regional and local exhibits at cultural centers, universities and festivals.

A true Boomer art center is the Portland's own Geezer Gallery which showcases art made by people over 60. The gallery evolved from research in art therapy for elders. Proceeds from artwork sales help fund senior art classes and art therapy for at-risk older people.

Similarly, Portland's emerging film scene offers film-lovers places to experience all genres of film as a viewer, a filmmaker or aspiring filmmaker.

Photographers also find inspiration in the area's diverse lush landscapes, coastline and wilderness areas and cityscapes great inspiration for the camera. Photographic expressions are found in photo galleries and centers and changing exhibitions throughout the area.

Arts festivals offer Boomer artists a place to display their creations and experience art in a fun, interesting venue.

See *APPENDIX B, Visual Arts Resources* on page 92 for listings of art, film and photography places, and resources and volunteer information.

If you're a beginner, other good starting points are art, film and photography clubs and organizations.

Art Volunteers

Many Boomers express their art-loving side in numerous volunteer roles that range from working in a cultural center to helping youth learn about art, film and photography. Most cultural non-profits – regardless of size – rely heavily on volunteers to make exhibits available.

Many are docents – people who act as guides and help bring exhibits to life. Volunteers, including those with certain specialties perform a wide variety of other volunteer tasks such as working with artists, musicians, staff and visitors. These may involve greeting visitors, assisting in a store, office work, and helping at previews, receptions, fundraisers and other events. Or discover ways to work with youth learning about art, film, and photography.

Festivals are another option for artsy volunteers. Art festivals often need lots of volunteers for day and weekend shows. Festivals offer a more relaxed atmosphere and volunteers usually enjoy the benefits of free passes and refreshments, with some fun thrown in. Tasks include construction and installation, setup, ushering and hosting, and on-the-ground festival coordination and outreach.

See *APPENDIX B, Visual Arts Resources* on page 92 for listings of art, film and photography places and resources, and volunteer information.

Arts and Culture Community Education Classes

You can also release your inner artist, writer, performer or musician or other aspiration through classes at museums, arts and performing arts centers and places like area community colleges and parks and recreation classes. *See APPENDIX L, Community Colleges Continuing Education* on page 167 and *Parks and Recreation Programs* on page 167 for lists of local community education programs.

CHAPTER 3: BUSINESS BUILDING: ENCORE ENTREPRENEURS

Boomers who release their inner entrepreneur and go into business are in good company. Boomers launch about one quarter of today's new businesses.

We're aptly labeled Encore Entrepreneurs, and those who go it alone are called "Solopreneurs."

We're driven to run our own shows. We're challenged by turning our expertise and knowledge into a business. We create new uses for our experience – consulting or writing for example. We turn hobbies and passions into successful "lifestyle businesses." We offer products or services that we find meaningful and that can make a difference to others.

Encores embrace technology and the Internet to start and operate our businesses. Add a touch of Portland's innovative culture and creative spirit, and Boomers find this an ideal time and place to go for their dreams.

Popular Business Options

While business opportunities are unlimited, examples of typical types of businesses Boomers engage in are:

- Consulting. Retirees return to employers or their industry as consultants.
- Lifestyle. Turn an interest such as jewelry-making, woodworking, collecting or blogging into a business.
- Online. Establish an Internet or a website business to sell products, services or information.
- Retail. Sell specialty products such as gifts, clothing and accessories, or food at a physical location.
- Teach, tutor or coach. Teach others what you know in pursuits such as music, art, writing, sailing, golf, fishing and many others.
- Hang your shingle. Provide professional services such as bookkeeping, accounting or personal services.

Getting Started

Want-to-be entrepreneurs often don't know where to begin. Owning even a simple business has many pieces and parts to address, starting with decisions such as business name, form of business, state registration and other legalities.

You need to determine specifics about your product or service, your customers and how to reach them, and how and where you will operate. Do you need employees? Physical equipment and supplies? What about office technology, a website, credit cards, bank accounts?

Not least among your decisions are how to finance and grow your business. All this leads to the necessity of a business plan.

Fortunately, abundant help and resources are available to Encores no matter where you are with your business.

Small Business Development Centers

SBDCs provide aspiring and current small business owners a variety of free business consulting and low-cost training services. Several local colleges and universities host SBDC activities including: Portland Community College, Mt. Hood Community College (Gresham), Clackamas Community College, and Washington State University (Vancouver).

State Business Offices

The official state websites of Oregon and Washington both provide easy-to-navigate information for businesses that operate within each state. Both sites detail steps to start a business and include practical and legal information about business names and structure, business plans, registrations, tax obligations, licenses, permits and ongoing requirements.

- Oregon Business Information Center

- Washington State, Start Your Business

Other Resources for Entrepreneurs

Other area organizations with resources that can help with launching and running a business include:

- Oregon Entrepreneurs Network. Resources for entrepreneurs in Portland, Beaverton, Vancouver, Hillsboro and other Metro areas. Membership.

- SCORE Portland. SCORE Vancouver. Sponsored by SBA, local chapters provide free mentoring and low-cost workshops. Both working and retired executives and business owners donate their time and expertise as business counselors.

Economic Development Organizations

As supporters of job creation, state and local economic development and chamber of commerce organizations provide access to resources and sponsor workshops for new business startups.

See *APPENDIX C: BUSINESS STARTUP RESOURCES* on page 97 for lists of city economic development and chamber of commerce organizations that provide resources for new and existing businesses.

CHAPTER 4: CARE FOR THE ENVIRONMENT

You love the outdoors and are willing to spend time caring for and helping preserve our natural assets. Oregon and Washington have a lot of environment to care about. In fact, we're known for it. Look at your favorite natural area, park, forest, river, lake, watershed or wildlife habitat and you'll find all types of groups who help preserve and protect it.

Options to give back to nature are plentiful. You'll find groups that adopt or friend their favorite community park, wildlife refuge, natural area, forest, river, wetlands or garden. Connect with advocates who speak up and teach about nature. Volunteer with city, county and parks departments who are eager to sign you up for park duty. Sign on with organizations in your own neighborhood that partner with cities and parks departments to keep parks healthy and safe.

Dig In, Clean Up, Party On!

Sign up for a work party. You can be part of a weekend or weekday (you're retired, remember) work party at a park, natural area, garden, or wildlife reserve. Unearth your boots, gloves and shovels to plant flowers, trees and

shrubs, pull weeds or build flower beds. Count birds and wildlife. Be an active learner and educate others on causes you are passionate about.

Organizations are flexible and will match your schedule to their activity. Choose a one-time project or clean-up, or be on a regular volunteer schedule. Get dirty working outside or skip the dirt and mud and work in an office or an outreach program. Take photos, write for blogs and websites. It all makes a difference.

You'll take away the satisfaction of connecting with Mother Earth, doing your part to keep the Northwest healthy, growing and green. Along the way you'll meet new people, and learn something new about our unique ecology. And don't forget how outdoor activity benefits brain health! It is so very win-win.

Here are three broad areas where you can dig deeper to find inspiration and information on the best places for you to join the green teams in your area.

Friend or Adopt a Park or Natural Area

Dedicated "friends of" and park stewardship groups throughout the area work to preserve local and community parks and natural areas. Often, they team up with city or county parks organizations. Park warriors like you participate in park planning, clean up and work parties, identifying problems,

and getting involved in park education and advocacy issues. Most friends groups are free or low-cost to join. Friends groups are perfect places to get your hands dirty, socialize and learn more about park ecology. And get outdoors! Look for activities you can do enjoy with kids and grandkids. Guaranteed you'll be digging around with young old people, like us.

Larger, one-time volunteer projects are offered through SOLVE.COM, a Portland non-profit that cleans, restores, educates and involves community through volunteerism. SOLVE Projects include clean-up, removal of invasive species, and planting, in various communities around Oregon.

See *APPENDIX D, Friend a Park or Natural Area* on page 98 for listings of parks, and city and county parks organizations with friends and volunteer groups in your county.

Ecological Preservation Groups

These volunteer groups tackle environmental preservation in expansive and dramatic spaces of rivers, watersheds, wetlands and wildlife habitats. For example, groups such as the Forest Park Conservancy focus on the ecological health of Forest Park, one of the country's largest urban parks with an extensive hiking trail system. Volunteer jobs at the Ridgefield National Wildlife Refuge in Washington range from conducting tours to habitat restoration. Friends of the Columbia Gorge works to preserve and a really sprawling, long, complicated space and protect the scenic natural wonder though work parties, discovery hikes and community education.

Volunteers at the Jackson Bottom Wetlands Preserve help at the education center and on crews that remove invasive plants, maintain trails, and work with marshes. Restoration projects at the Lower Columbia Estuary Partnership may appeal to those who like to canoe or kayak to a work site.

Organizations such as the Nature Conservancy of Oregon and Nature Conservancy of Washington sponsor restoration projects that benefit natural areas in both states.

See listings of organizations in *APPENDIX D, Protecting Ecological Areas* beginning on page 101 to find your ideal volunteer activity if you're passionate about sustaining and protecting sensitive ecological areas.

Advocacy and Education

If your passion is sharing knowledge, many environmental organizations welcome outreach and education volunteers. Many ecological preservation groups advocate for their area in public and political forums. Organizations such as the Oregon Sierra Club get involved in the nitty gritty of Environmental Impact Statements and in influencing public policy decisions – legislative, administrative, legal, and electoral. Oregon Wild actively communicates with the public regarding political issues involving the public wildlands, wildlife and waters.

Outreach programs of several groups involve workshops, classes and models of environmental preservation in action at their site. For example, Vancouver Watersheds Alliance community programs support care of water resources. Rewild Portland educates the public on earth-based arts, traditions and technologies through workshops, programs and community-building events.

Other non-profits such as Columbia Springs bring environmental education to the community through on-site education programs in schools and at community events.

See *APPENDIX D, Environmental Advocacy and Education Organizations* on page 103 to find a list of organizations with volunteer activities in environmental outreach.

CHAPTER 5: CAREER ENCORES

While many Boomers eagerly trade jobs and career for a leisure retirement, others opt to stay in the workforce. An increasing number want or need to work for the money. Others do because they flat out enjoy their jobs, the daily routine and their daily contact with co-workers. Not to mention that they find their work satisfying and feel valued. Sometimes, it's just hard to let go.

Turning Points and Second Chances

Retirement age for many Boomers is a turning point. It's finally time to look elsewhere for a more meaningful career or job, or a better schedule or setup. Some prefer a gradual transition out of their jobs, working out part-time or consulting deals.

Still others are ready for a second chance to do what they love. For them, it's now-or-never time to realize an entrepreneurial dream and turn skills, experience and interests into a business or do independent work.

Change Careers, Profession or Situation

Popular stay-in-the-workforce options among Boomers are:

- Transitioning to another role within an organization, applying expertise to areas such as training or mentoring.

- Shifting to a flexible or part-time schedule, or working from a home office.

- Moving to a similar position at a different organization within the same industry.

- Taking business skills and experience to a favorite non-profit.

- Seeking out a new batch of education or training to pivot to an entirely different career, profession or industry.

Where to Start the Process

Either within or outside your current situation, a good job search involves research and networking – activities Boomers know well. The process starts by evaluating skills, experience and expertise and defining an "ideal" job. Among the many parts of ideal are hours, work environment, location, work culture, interaction, projects and compensation.

Research the types of industries and organizations that would be a good fit. Learn more through internet searches, talking with friends, acquaintances, or people within the organization. Take advantage of the tools, resources and people available to you, many at no or low cost.

Today's online world delivers job search guides, checklists and other tools to your desktop. From building a resume to interviewing, to networking, to researching, it is all out there.

Resources for Career Change

Hands-on job seekers enroll in live classes and seminars at community colleges; many also coach. Companies and industry groups, and even AARP, sponsor job fairs and online job fairs and career classes.

Experts agree that networking – a skill Boomers naturally excel at – is the key to finding a new gig. It's easy to spread the word among networks of friends, acquaintances, former employers, workout buddies and others. They are eager to help. Social media such as LinkedIn and Facebook are good ways to connect; use them in ways appropriate for you and your current employment situation.

Another interesting option is the Encore Fellows program. Encore Fellows matches seasoned professionals with local nonprofits in need of professional expertise for year-long, half-time paid assignments.

The following are organizations with websites that Boomers can tap into to find and land a new job.

- AARP. Portland Jobs, Work & Job Resources. Job hunting articles and links to job hunting sites, including niche sites and social media.

- AARP Tek Academy. An online connection to job search tools and online career fairs.

- Clackamas Community College. Classes and job search resources. Career and technical programs for career changers.

- Clark College. Classes and job search resources. Career and technical programs for career changers.

- Job search websites: Career Builder, Career One Stop, Indeed, Monster. Search for job openings by location and job type.

- Life by Design NW. Training programs on how to successfully navigate work-life transitions and plan for meaningful retirement.

- Mt. Hood Community College. Career and technical programs for career changers.

- MACs list. Online source for jobs in Portland. Lists jobs, internships, volunteer jobs and events with emphasis on non-profits.

- Portland Community College. Classes and job search resources. Career and technical programs for career changers.

CHAPTER 6: COMMUNITY SERVICE

Next phase for many is a time to give back and make our communities better places to live now and in the future.

Retiring Boomers have more time on their hands and feel the need to give back. We bring a lifetime of experience and skills that many organizations and causes need and value. Instead of looking for being paid, Boomers now look to pay back in their communities.

Opportunities for Boomers in community service are abundant. Our community cares deeply about the needs of health-challenged, less fortunate and underserved populations. We want to help people out of the mainstream who may be homeless and hungry, or need other help.

Many of these community service organizations are non-profit and almost all-volunteer. Many are grass-roots community groups and others are sponsored by churches and civic groups. Many people – like you – start and run them.

Service Organizations

Look for a general category below that interests you and the types of volunteers they typically need, then turn to the page listing the organizations in that category.

- **Addictions and Mental Health**. A wide variety of organizations serve the community through mental health treatment, education and support for adults, families and children. Volunteers perform in many support roles such as mentoring, answering calls, development, fundraising, communication, teaching and helping at events. See *APPENDIX E, Addictions and Mental Health* on page 106 for descriptive list.

- **Disability Services**. These organizations support adults and children with disabilities to help people realize their potential and provide opportunities in areas such as housing, recreation, fitness, daily living, transportation and socializing. Volunteers assist with programs, camp activities, work parties, social events, fundraising, learning and education, transportation, fundraising and administrative support. See *APPENDIX E, Disability Services* on page 107 for a descriptive list.

- **Emergency Services**. Emergency food, shelter and other services are provided to individuals, including adults and families, by a variety of non-profit, faith-based and other agencies. Volunteers assist in shelters, food pantries, clothing rooms, thrift stores; they pack and serve meals, help with care tasks, drive, teach, and perform many other roles. See *APPENDIX E, Emergency Services* on page 109 for a descriptive list.

- **Family and Social Services**. Many area organizations serve families through programs that address families dealing with social issues such as abuse, relationship issues, illness and financial problems. Volunteers help with client care tasks and education and work in shelters and offices. See *APPENDIX E, Family and Social Services* on page 110 for a descriptive list.

- **Food Banks and Gardens**. Food pantries provide food for low-income individuals and families and people who are homeless. Fresh food is grown and harvested at several area gardens and provided through food banks. Food bank volunteers help unpack, repackage, sort and box food and serve clients. Garden and farm volunteers help plant, weed, harvest and deliver fruits and vegetables to food banks. They also build gardens and teach people how to grow their own food. See *APPENDIX E, Food Banks and Gardens* on page 112 for a descriptive list.

- **Hunger and Homeless Services**. Resources for individuals and families who are homeless include overnight shelters, meals, clothing, health care, training, transitional programs and many other services provided by non-profits, faith-based organizations and government agencies. Volunteers always are needed help in shelters, prepare meals, interact with clients, help with childcare, work in clothing and food rooms, teach and reach out to the community and help maintain buildings, facilities and yards. See *APPENDIX E, Hunger and Homeless Services* on page 113 for a descriptive list.

- **Youth Programs**. A variety of programs for all ages of youth offer opportunities to learn and grow through sports, reading and writing, games, arts and crafts, music, outdoor activities – many with emphasis on underserved populations. Several programs address needs of children dealing with difficult family situations and health issues. Volunteers help mentor, teach and coach children. They help with trips and events, work in outreach and with fundraising. See *APPENDIX E, Youth Programs* on page 116 for a descriptive list.

CHAPTER 7: CYCLING: RIDE, BOOMERS, RIDE!

Ready to cycle into your next phase of leisure living? It's a popular way to experience outdoor activity with family and friends, exercise or to just enjoy the calming peace of a solo ride.

The good news for you is that you need look no further to find one of the country's top five bicycle friendly cities. Cycling goes beyond popular here in Portland – it's embedded into our culture.

Lots of options for Boomers. Learn to trail ride. Cycle around town in bike lanes. Or in your own community.

Thanks to bicycle advocacy groups and Department of Transportation programs, city and county planning accommodates and encourages bicycling both as recreation and transportation.

Through its Bicycle Portland website, Portland Department of Transportation (PDOT) provides resources on riding in Portland, bicycle news and events, maps, and other resources. Through the PDOT Senior Cyclist Program, adults new to cycling can find information, a supportive setting, and classes to get back on the bike.

Other places for bicycling information are the websites of:

- Metro Biking Resources. Visit the oregonmetro.gov for maps, videos and other resources for cyclists including bike-TriMet transportation options, road hazard information, "tricky spot" tips, and more links to resources in the cycling community.

- Rails to Trails Conservancy TrailLink.com, an on-line source for 30,000 trail maps, searchable by location.

Places to Bike, Maps

Q: Where in Cycle-landia can you ride?

A: Nearly anywhere around Portland. In neighborhoods, within 100s of miles of bike commuter lanes, over bridges, in downtowns, along bike paths, and on rails-to-trails paths. Over rolling countryside hills. At cycling events, with clubs, with people of all ages. On designated forest trails. There's practically no place you can't cycle in Portland.

See *APPENDIX F, Cycling Places and Resources by County* on page 121 for a lineup of cycling resources in Clackamas, Clark, Multnomah and Washington Counties.

Cycling Clubs, Meetups, Annual Events

No matter where you hang your helmet, or whether you are a recreational to competitive cyclist, there's a club or Meetup group for you.

Meetups area popular option for Boomers seeking all things outdoors, including cycling. Meetups are groups formed by individuals around a common or multiple interests. Joining is generally free or inexpensive and gives you access to the meet-up's scheduled activities.

As expected in cycle-crazy Portland, if you can imagine it, there's a bike Meetup for it. At any given time, you'll find 10-15 meet-up groups for all abilities, ages, and interest, in all parts of the metro. Some recreational, others hard-core serious. Some ride and tour year-round. You'll also find training rides for fundraising groups such as Arthritis Foundation Tour de Cure Oregon/SW WA and the Arthritis Foundation Classic Cycling Group-Oregon.

Meetups come, go and change. To find what's current, go to Meetup.com for Portland Meetups and enter your interest such as outdoor, cycling, etc. Meetup descriptions will tell you about the activity or interest, who it is appropriate for, a schedule of meetings, and what part of town it's located in.

If you want to be surrounded by hundreds, or even thousands of your new best friends, register for a cycling event. For current listings see Oregon Bicycle Ride Calendar, the bikingbis.com list of bike rides; bikeportland.org/calendar events by month; and events12.com/portland calendar.

See *APPENDIX F, Cycling Clubs, Meetups and Events* on page 122 for lists of clubs, Meetup groups and popular annual events for cyclists.

CHAPTER 8: FITNESS AND HEALTHY LIVING

Boomers heading into their next chapter want to be healthy and fit enough to enjoy it. And the secret formula is really no secret – exercise and diet are the best "magic pills" we have for a healthy quality of life.

Being healthy and fit helps improves our mental fitness, balance, stamina, flexibility, strength, mobility and ability to ward off disease.

Exercise is essential because it strengthens our hearts and nourishes our brains. Boomers who exercise regularly feel better and can do more.

Already healthy and fit? Try a new activity to help keep you on track. Or, if you had a sedentary, butt-in-the seat job, look for a gradual program to start exercising. Try these three steps:

- Step One – Fit fitness activity into your life by thinking about what activities you enjoy or always wanted to try. Do you like the outdoors? Do you prefer being indoors for fitness classes or water exercise? Always wanted to dance? Golf? Garden, do yard work? Walk the dog?

- Step Two – Next think about your goals? More energy, stamina to keep up with your spouse, friends, kids, or grandkids? Weight loss? Better body image? Improved quality of life? Better sleep? Make new friends?

- Step Three – Scope out your options. Fitness opportunities – outdoor and indoor – surround Boomers in our own communities. Choices of places, programs and classes for your fitness quest are endless. Add the huge benefit, yes benefit, of age – many fitness activities are either free or discounted for adults and older adults. Look for them. Two of them – Silver&Fit® and SilverSneakers® – no cost fitness programs included in many senior health plans and group retirement plans.

Now, check out our rundown of Boomer-popular, fun and readily available fitness options below.

Fitness Options

Important advice from fitness experts is to continually challenge yourself in some small way and set goals. Goals can be a cycling distance, walking in an event, taking on a ski or snowshoe trail.

Walk, Hike, Cycle or Ski to Fitness

The easiest way to start a fitness program is by walking. Get a good pair of walking shoes and comfortable socks and workout clothes. Join a group of like-minded people. Or find a walking buddy to keep you both on track.

Head out in your own neighborhood, taking in the scenery, the people and neighborhood parks and gardens. Step it up and venture to other

neighborhoods. Or check out walking and hiking trails around town. Join a walking group or Meetup. Check a neighborhood's walk score (walkscore.com/score) which tells you how easy and safe it is to walk to shopping, activities and transportation.

In winter, extend your local-motion to snow sports – join other Boomers in fitness activities such as cross-country skiing and snowshoeing. For more about resources, clubs and activities for all abilities, see:

- Outdoor Clubs list, see *APPENDIX G, Outdoor Clubs* on page 125.

- Hiking and Walking Resources, see *APPENDIX J: HIKING AND WALKING RESOURCES* on page 145.

- *CHAPTER 7: CYCLING: RIDE, BOOMERS, RIDE!* on page 29.

Jogging and Running – Oregon's Legacy

One guess – What state originated jogging?

Another – What age group advanced it to a health craze?

(Answers: Oregon and the Baby Boomers, of course!)

Are you still jogging along, no doubt a bit slower than you did in the 60s, 70s and 80s? Or is jogging/running for fitness on your bucket list? How about a 5K? 10K? Marathon? Aerobic activities such as jogging and running raise your heart rate and are important to good heart health and brain fitness.

Start with a good pair of running shoes, comfortable socks and workout clothes (no cotton!) and take off. You can jog practically anywhere. Prefer some company? Show up for group runs sponsored by a club or local running store. Most clubs welcome all abilities and you'll have plenty of company no matter what your pace.

Put a 5K or 10K event on the calendar. Running events attract hundreds and even thousands of joggers, runners and walkers of all shapes, sizes and abilities. Many Boomers jog with their grandkids. Most races are family friendly with kids' races and walks. What's not to like about them?

It's also wise to look into group training sessions that help prepare you for a race. For more information, see:

- runningintheusa.com. A website where you can search for local event schedules by city. Find one and sign up. Register on line.

- Running Clubs, a list of area age-friendly running clubs, in *APPENDIX G, Running Clubs*, on page 126.

Just Keep Swimming

Boomer swimmers love the gentle all-body workout water exercise gives them, making swimming a popular year-around fitness activity. Lap swims, lessons and water exercise are available at aquatic centers, parks and recreation facilities, community colleges and public swimming pools.

See *APPENDIX G, Aquatics Centers* on page 126 for a list of area aquatic facilities.

Play Tennis or Pickleball, Anyone?

Tennis and pickleball are each fun, fit-friendly and social activities that go beyond just moving exercise. Swatting a ball across a net pulls in your brain,

connects eyes to racquet hand. To keep relationships harmonious, you can partner with, instead of against, a spouse or friend. It's easy to get lessons through many community programs and find other Boomer players at activities like the PTC Senior Mixers sponsored by Portland Parks & Recreation, which combines tennis and socializing.

Pickleball has become a wildly popular sport among Boomers. Much like tennis, players swat balls back and forth on a smaller court, over a net. A solid paddle and a ball similar to a whiffle ball over a shorter net slow things down. For more on area pickleball schedules, resources and facilities see:

- The Pickleball Press, a local Facebook page with links to pickleball schedules and places.

- Tennis and Pickleball Places and Activities, see list in *APPENDIX G, Pickleball and Tennis* on page 127.

Join a Senior or Community Center

Health and fitness – both physical and mental – are a main focus of some 50 senior centers, community centers and YMCAs in the Portland area that gear activities to different ages, abilities and interests.

Senior centers offer services and activities to help seniors live, learn, thrive, and socialize. Depending on the community, Boomers can take advantage of fitness classes in strength training, dance, aerobics, Tai Chi, Yoga and other popular exercises. Many offer classes in lifestyle, health and nutrition. Many post have websites with schedules of free or low-cost classes. See *APPENDIX P, Community and Senior Centers*, on page 182 for a list of area centers.

More Choices: Community College and Parks & Rec

In addition to community centers, boomers can sign up for fitness classes offered by parks and recreation departments of their cities and community colleges. Because college classes and web page locations change seasonally, you may have to dig around some websites for a current catalog. See *APPENDIX G: COMMUNITY COLLEGES AND PARKS & REC, YMCA* on page 128 for lists of community programs offering senior fitness activities.

Find Healthy Lifestyles at Healthcare Organizations

Many area healthcare organizations offer health-related classes and events to their members and to the community at large. Some have online classes and videos. Ongoing, popular classes are healthy eating, fitness and exercise, weight management, smoking cessation, healthy lifestyles, support groups, reducing stress, pain management, depression, yoga and many other health topics related to seniors and retirees.

Classes are listed on the websites of the following organizations; search for the site's classes page.

- Adventist Health, adventisthealth.org/nw
- Kaiser Permanente, kp.org
- Legacy Health, legacyhealth.org
- PeaceHealth Southwest, peacehealth.org
- Providence Health, oregon.providence.org
- Tuality Healthcare, tuality.org

Fitness Activities Meetups

No matter what your fitness level or interest, there's a club or Meetup group for you. Meetups are formed by individuals around a common or multiple interests, in this case, walking, hiking or fitness. Joining is either free or inexpensive and gives you online access to the meetup's scheduled activities.

See *APPENDIX G: Fitness Clubs and Meetups* on page 129 for a list of groups that sponsor a variety of fitness activities.

CHAPTER 9: GARDENING: TEND A GARDEN

Got a little dirt under your nails? Have a need to pluck weeds and water flowers? If so, there's probably a gardener growing in you!

Portland gardeners recognize constant rain as an ideal growing climate for gardens of all sizes and shapes. Look around. Seems like everyone either wants to start or spend more time in a garden for good reason. Gardening grounds us. Clears our brains. Expresses our creativity. Gives us solitude. And makes us patient.

If you're a Boomer gardener or want-to-be, it's time to unearth gloves and shovels, and get to the garden of your choice. Portland is garden friendly to beginners and experts alike – gardeners love to share their knowledge.

Start by venturing out to see all the luscious gardens that bless our area (and beyond). Then bring your inspiration back in photographs to start applying those ideas to your own yard, containers or balcony.

Enjoy Public and Demonstration Gardens

Whether you're a beginner, expert, or appreciator, you'll discover endless ways to enjoy gardens in metro Portland.

Gather inspiration by wandering through colorful rose gardens in Portland's

Washington Park, Ladd's Addition, Peninsula Park or Vancouver's Esther Short Park. Area gardens range from the expansive Oregon Garden south of Portland to exquisite Japanese and Chinese Gardens, to native species in Hoyt Arboretum and Leach Botanical Gardens.

Delight in bursts of color and species in the Crystal Springs Rhododendron garden. Go north of Vancouver to collect ideas from the themed and demonstration gardens at the Wildlife Botanical Gardens. Or discover smaller, tucked-away gardens such Bishop's Close Elk Rock Garden or the Roger Clematis Garden in West Linn. And ask plenty of questions.

Several area demonstration gardens offer the latest on new plants, trees, and growing techniques. You'll find sites that focus on fruit growing, organic gardening and gardens as wildlife habitat, as well as techniques to manage factors such as water usage, soil enhancement and safety.

See *APPENDIX H, Public and Demonstration Gardens* on page 130, for list by county of gardens to enjoy, or join a friends group or volunteer team.

Volunteer at a Public Garden

All public gardens need and welcome volunteers of all skill levels and interests. Great for beginners! Tasks range from hands-on planting, weeding,

and mulching, to helping out at special events, or working in gift shops, or offices. You can show up at one-time work parties or join others in ongoing year-round maintenance. Some branch out into community projects. For example, volunteer gardeners at the Portland Japanese Gardens help out in a school program engaging underserved youth.

Take volunteering a step further and join a group that adopts and maintains their favorite public garden. Some require that you become a member.

See *APPENDIX H, Public and Demonstration Gardens* on page 130, for list by county of gardens to enjoy, or join a friends group or volunteer team.

Community Gardens

When you enjoy growing things, but lack the space to plant your personality, it's time to discover community gardens. You'll enjoy the satisfaction of beautiful flowers or healthy vegetables, and meet others with the same interests. Share tips, seeds, and even recipes.

Most communities offer residents plots, and various gardening equipment and services for gardeners. Many offer classes, gardening tips and expert help from volunteer and master gardeners.

On the community service side, gardeners volunteer their talents to help low income grow their own food, or volunteer time in food growing orchards and gardens which donate fresh food to food banks. Some offer tool-sharing.

Garden volunteers interested in community service may volunteer at organizations such as Growing Gardens. This organization helps people grow their own food. Volunteers help build organic, raised bed vegetable gardens in back yards, front yards, side yards and balconies.

See *APPENDIX H, Community Gardens* on page 133 for a list of area community gardens.

Garden Clubs

To get the real dirt on gardening, try a garden club. Garden clubs are a fun, social way to learn and share information and enhance the beauty of your community. Garden clubs sponsor regular guest speakers, workshops, plant shows, plant sales and exchanges and garden tours. Some clubs offer scholarships for aspiring horticulturalists as well as donate goods and time to local charities.

Members also maintain flower beds in their cities, and encourage the appreciation of wildflowers, birds, and insects and the wise use of natural resources. Moreover members share the fellowship of like-minded men and women.

Look through the list of Garden Clubs on page 134 to find one in your area. All welcome aspiring green thumbs, and are eager to help and share their knowledge. Most are affiliated with either the Oregon State Federation of Garden Clubs, or the Washington State Federation of Garden Clubs.

Gardening Classes, Workshops and Seminars

Gardening for most of us is evolutionary – there's always more to learn. Discover new design, seeds, soils, watering, plants, color, harvest – it goes on

and on. And there's no shortage of places to learn more, get advice, attend classes and seminars and hang out with other gardeners.

To really dig into gardening, attend Master Gardener classes offered throughout the metro area. Programs at Oregon State University and the University of Washington cater to the serious gardener. Master Gardeners in turn share their knowledge through gardening-related demonstrations, lectures, seminars and workshops in communities throughout the area.

Other options are community education gardening classes generally held in spring and fall. Search for gardening classes offered at area community colleges. Area nurseries and garden centers also hold gardening classes and hands-on workshops.

Home and Garden shows are still another source of classes and workshops to inspire and educate gardeners. See *APPENDIX H, Events and Shows* on page 136 for a list of area gardening events.

Also, contact a garden club. Many open their classes to the public. Community gardens also sponsor classes for those who want a healthy, thriving, and successful planting. See *APPENDIX H, Garden Clubs* on page 134 for a list of area garden clubs.

Like to share your knowledge? Contact your favorite garden club, gardens, community college, senior center or nurseries to teach a class.

See the list of *APPENDIX H, Classes, Workshops and Seminars* on page 136 for a list of places to learn more about gardening.

Green Thumb Meetup Groups

Boomer gardeners should check out Meetup groups. Meetups are formed by individuals around a common or multiple interests, in this case, gardening. Joining is either free or inexpensive and gives you on-line access to the Meetup's scheduled activities.

Examples of gardening Meetups are:

- Abba's Garden
- Clark County Gardening
- NW Home Gardening
- Sharing Garden Ideas, Seeds and Plants
- Sprout Growing Gardens and Community

Meetups come, go and change. To find what's current, go to Meetups.com and search for your city, then your interest such as gardening, bees, roses, etc. The Meetup website describes the activity or interest, who it is appropriate for, time/date of meetings and activities, and what part of town it's located in. Sign up and show up.

CHAPTER 10: HEALTH AND HEALING VOLUNTEERS

Boomers who have retired from healthcare careers, or those who are interested in healthcare, can find a wide assortment of places and ways to offer their help in an area with many volunteer opportunities. Your

involvement is needed and welcomed by all types of medical and healthcare organizations, including...

Community Healthcare

Non-profit community health clinics bring low-cost or free healthcare to underserved, disadvantaged and low-income populations, minorities, elderly, families, children and others.

Often working with limited budgets, these organizations depend heavily on volunteers with medical and non-medical skills for day-to-day operations. On the medical side, professionals such as doctors, nurses, clinicians, dentists, technicians are always needed, as are volunteers who serve as medical advocates, screeners, interpreters and translators. Also welcome is background in office support, technology and computer services, graphic design, communication, and fundraising support.

See *APPENDIX I, Community Healthcare Organizations* on page 139 for a list of organizations.

Community Mental Health

Community Mental Health non-profits serve the mentally ill, as well as adults and children with addictions. Mental health organizations are supported by private organizations, faith-based organizations, and city and county governments. The types of specialties they represent include family and individual mental health and addictions.

Volunteer opportunities range from mental health professionals and those who assist them, to childcare, education, manning crisis phone lines and socializing in residential facilities. Volunteers also work in office settings, gardens, thrift stores and at special events.

See *APPENDIX I, Community Mental Health Programs* on page 140 for a list.

Health-based Organizations

These familiar organizations focus on advancing cures and treatment of a specific condition or disease, and services and support for people and families affected by the disease. Among the best known are the American Cancer Society, American Heart Association, MS Society and Alzheimer's Association, all with local chapters.

Boomers often choose organizations that speak to their hearts – the disease or condition may affect them or their families or friends.

The work of many non-profits focuses on various children's diseases and conditions such as cancer, autism, kidney disease and cerebral palsy.

Organizations seek volunteers in roles that support their mission and activities. In general, volunteers help provide services, educate the public and raise money. They also work in office roles, maintain databases, file and answer phones. On the communications side, volunteers may help with websites, social media, graphic design, photography and writing blogs.

See *APPENDIX I, Health-Based Support Organizations* on page 141 for a list.

Hospice and End of Life Care

Volunteers provide important services to hospice organizations and the people they serve. Whether providing companionship to a person in the final months and weeks of life, offering support to family and caregivers, or helping with community outreach and fundraising, the contributions of volunteers are essential to the important work provided by hospice programs.

Every hospice relies on volunteer support to provide excellent end-of-life care to each patient and family. In fact, Medicare requires that 5% of patient care time be provided by volunteers.

See *APPENDIX I, Hospice and End of Life Care* on page 143 for a list facilities and resources.

Hospitals and Medical Centers

By this time in our lives, most Boomers are no strangers to medical centers and hospitals. We often recall the kindness of hospital volunteers who showed us to a room or brought us flowers or a newspaper. Volunteers bring joy to people during what can be stressful times. Most hospitals offer volunteer positions throughout their operations.

Duties of hospital volunteers vary widely depending upon the facility. Volunteers may work in staff reception areas and gift shops, file and retrieve documents and mails, take out trash, clean up after nurses and doctors, provide administrative backup, assist with research, help visitors, visit with patients or transport various small items like flowers, medical records, lab specimens and drugs from unit to unit.

Other "advanced volunteers" are those who work on health care teams and are given special training to work with patients. They are more common in large hospitals, particularly university-affiliated and teaching hospitals.

See *APPENDIX I, Hospitals and Medical Centers* on page 144 for a list of area medical centers.

CHAPTER 11: HIKING AND WALKING: TAKE A HIKE!

Why are hiking and walking the Boomer exercises of choice? Easy – they are abundantly good for you and opportunities are as plentiful as Northwest rain.

Just look at the bookshelves overflowing with guides for newbie and experienced trekkers alike.

Multi-taskers can bundle walking with other leisure goals and hobbies. Pare down that paunch, give your spouse space, feed your brain or listen to birds. Explore communities beyond your own; discover out-of-the-way parks, trails and fun little towns. Surround yourself with real forests and mountains, rivers and wetlands. Make hikes and walks an excuse to see more of your family and friends, or meet new people. Or for some me time.

Hiking Destinations Around Portland

Gather your friends, pick a destination, then download a map from the Portland Hikes section of the on-line *Oregon Hikers Field Guide*. See *APPENDIX J, Hikes Through Natural, Wildlife and Scenic Areas* on page 145 for a listing of hikes by county, city, and section of town, summarized and published with permission of the *Field Guide*.

In snow season, head to the hills and mountains, to any of dozens of cross-country ski and snowshoe trails listed at Trails.com, pick your state, activity and zoom in to a trail.

And you needn't always traipse about a forest, park, or mountain trail to reap the great health, aesthetic and social benefits. Go to any number of interesting urban or historic hiking routes. You're surrounded by walkable neighborhoods ranging from the downtown stylish, to old European influenced hillside homes, to grand old back-in-the-day neighborhoods.

One place to find about-town walks is by visiting walkingoregon.com for route maps and descriptions of walks in various Oregon towns developed by the Oregon Volkssport clubs.

Neighborhood Walks

Discover a fascinating interblending of communities with natural areas, as well as old and new commercial and office areas. Neighborhoods that transition from burbie housing to undeveloped natural areas. Lots of river walks. You'll delight in a diverse selection of urban-suburban-boondocks destinations.

Make *Walking Routes* another Favorite. It's an online reference to bike and walk routes in Greater Portland and Vancouver, courtesy of Portland Bureau of Transportation. Thanks also to the PDOT website for free Bike+Walk Maps. Just find the site and click on the map area you want. In Vancouver, check out the parks and recreation maps of urban and rural walks.

The Metro Walk There! website page describes and maps walking routes in different sections of Portland metro. The Explore section of the Intertwine.com website also provides maps and descriptions of parks, trails and natural areas throughout the region.

Try a Club or Meetup Group

Throughout the metro, age-friendly outdoor clubs and meetups welcome non-members to try them. Most offer different levels of activity and are a perfect way to meet liked-minded Boomers. Many schedule activities during weekdays at times preferred by Boomer-retiree members and guests. Many

clubs offer multi-activities such as hiking, walking, mountaineering, snowshoeing, cycling, kayaking and backpacking.

Meetups are formed by individuals on Meetup.com around a common or multiple interests, in this case, outdoors, hiking, or walking. Joining is either free or inexpensive and gives you online access to the Meetup's scheduled activities.

See *APPENDIX J, Outdoor Hike, Walk, Snow Sports Groups* on page 151 for a list of multi-activity outdoor clubs.

Community College and City Recreation Programs

Browse the catalogs of community colleges and city parks and recs for a wide variety of seasonal outdoor senior programs and walk and hike activities. Online sign-up is easy. Popular among Boomers are hikes, walks, walk tours, nature and historic tours, nature center visits and similar activities.

See *APPENDIX J, Community Education, Parks & Rec Programs* on page 152 for a list of those offering outdoor programs.

Walk in a Community Event

Choose from literally dozens of walking and walker-friendly events; some are multi-sport, multi-distance family events such as running races. Walk and multiply the benefits – your registration supports community causes and you get exercise, camaraderie and freebies. Plus, they are fun!

See *APPENDIX J, Walk Friendly Community Events* on page 153 for a list of area walking events and walker friendly events in.

Two sites that list current events are:

- Events12.com/Portland. Monthly listings and links to area events, festivals, and things to do.

- Running in the USA.com. Select your state and city, month and/or distance to get a current list of events. Most running events welcome walkers.

Art and Cultural Meanderings

Here's another I-gotta'-walk idea: Walk with a touch of culture. Log your

miles when you show up for "first-something" art walks, or stroll through any of several area monthly or seasonal art walks. You'll also get your steps in on guided or self-guided tours of historical sites, homes, buildings, farms and gardens. Similarly, take advantage of events at expansive walk-around attractions in places such as Oregon Gardens and Oregon Zoo, as well as community sponsored brew and wine walks.

See *APPENDIX J, Art and Cultural Meanderings* on page 154 for a list of artsy, cultural destinations to walk your way through.

CHAPTER 12: HOBBIES: GET ONE

What do you like to do, make, collect or play? Research tells us that engaging in a creative hobby tops the list of best activities for your brain. Maybe, now that we have the opportunity, it's time to move that hobby up the list.

Are you ready to express yourself with oil or water color? Start a 60s record collection, make jewelry, take photos, drag out old bins of scrapbook material? What about restoring – toys, a car, furniture?

You might like to visit quaint antique shops of antiques. Sell stuff on eBay. Write a blog, memoir or your family history. Learn the guitar or mandolin. Create or expand a garden. Or, express your out-of-the-box side with rock balancing, pigeon racing, blacksmithing or beekeeping.

A hobby can come from any interest – something you make, build, create, collect, fix, read or learn about. Maybe it's a sport, art, music, books, history, an outdoor pursuit. You can do it by yourself or in a group. There are endless possibilities – see our list of hobbies in *APPENDIX K: HOBBY IDEAS FOR YOU!* assembled from others around the internet on page 155.

Where to Start

Searching in our digital world brings information and how-to videos right to your computer or phone screen. Search by hobby name and city and see what pops up. Other good places are stores that supply hobby materials.

Places that Boomers can look to start or expand a hobby:

- **Community College Continuing Education programs**. Community colleges offer classes on a wide spectrum of life-long learning interests including art, music, cooking, dancing, photography, reading, language, woodworking, sports, and more. Find out more in print or online catalogs.
  - o Clackamas Community College (clackamas.edu). Open Community Ed catalog. 62+ may qualify for senior discount.
  - o Clark College (ecd.clark.edu).
  - o Mt. Hood Community College (mhcc.edu/). Senior discounts.
  - o Portland Community College (pcc.edu/community).
- **Community and Senior Centers**. These friendly places are built around hobbies such as reading, dancing, card playing, arts and crafts, exercise, fitness, computers and technology and day trips. Groups always welcome

beginners and are eager to share their knowledge. See *APPENDIX P, Community and Senior Centers* on page 182 to find one in your area.

- **Libraries**. In addition to hobby books and media – libraries sponsor a variety of programs, usually free, on all sorts of topics. Or you can suggest one, or even teach one. See *APPENDIX L, Public Libraries by County* on page 163 to find one in your community.

- **Clubs, Meetups and Social Groups** People in most of these groups share a common interest. From arts, hobbies and crafts, to writing, culture, DIY, and many other activities, Meetups might be the place to look. Start research for hobby groups here – *CHAPTER 18: POSTIVE CONNECTIONS, SOCIAL CLUBS, GROUPS* on page 61.

- **Parks and Recreation Programs**. Check the quarterly activities calendars of area parks and recreation programs for adult and senior group classes and activities such as creative arts, crafts, music, dance, bird watching, outdoor activities, games, history and many more.

  ○ Hillsboro Parks & Recreation (hillsboro-oregon.gov). Open activities guide, includes Senior Activities.

  ○ North Clackamas Parks and Recreation District (ncprd.com). Open Discovery Guide.

  ○ Oregon City Parks & Recreation (orcity.org/parksandrecreation). Classes through Pioneer Senior Center.

  ○ Portland Parks & Recreation (portlandoregon.gov/parks). Senior Recreation Catalog.

  ○ Tualatin Hills Park & Recreation District (thprd.org). Activities Guide.

  ○ Vancouver Parks & Recreation (cityofvancouver.us/parksrec). Catalog Activity Guide. 50 and Better Activities.

  ○ Wilsonville Parks & Recreation (wilsonvilleparksandrec.com). Open Activity Guide. Active Adults program.

Depending on your interests, other ways to pursue leisure hobbies are classes at cultural institutions such as art galleries, museums, literary organizations and programs sponsored by outdoor organizations and hobby supply stores. For more places to discover and pursue your passion, browse through *CHAPTER 2: ARTS & CULTURE* on page 11; *CHAPTER 4: CARE FOR THE ENVIRONMENT* on page 21; *CHAPTER 9: GARDENING: TEND A GARDEN* on page 35; *CHAPTER 16: MUSEUMS AND HISTORICAL SITES* on page 57; and *CHAPTER 19: THE GREAT OUTDOORS* on page 63.

CHAPTER 13: LEARN, RESEARCH, READ

There's no limit to what you can learn, and there's no limit to where you can find what you want. The Portland area is rich with educational opportunity that transcends degree chasing and focuses on more expansive interests that you might never find in a traditional classroom.

Learn Something New

What is challenging your mind in your world?

Understanding current events, some historical curiosity, some unexplored mystery of life? Now that you have more time available, your interests may turn to learning more about topics that fascinate you in your community, state or country.

"We learn from each other and never stop learning" is a familiar Boomer Mantra, and it perfectly expresses the passion members have for the Senior Studies Institute (SSI). Year-round, senior learners enjoy a variety of speakers ranging from former Governor Barbara Roberts and author Brian Doyle, to local old-camera enthusiast Ralph London.

Sponsored by Portland Community College, SSI is one of many lively senior learning forums you can find at a variety of education venues around town.

Several of Portland's public and private colleges and universities invite the public to attend student and facility lectures, classes, music and arts performances that enhance their curriculum.

While Internet and TV screens bring the world to your easy chair, it's far more interesting and fun to mix it up with others who share your interests. There are many low- or no-cost forums in your community to learn more about topics that fascinate you. See *APPENDIX L, University Lectures and Forms Open to the Public* on page 162.

More Learning Places

Among other places to "never stop learning" are retiree organizations, many of which hold regular member with guest speakers on current topics. Check the website of your former employer or their retiree website.

Community colleges offer credit and non-credit community education classes on a wide spectrum of learning interests. Find out more in seasonal catalogs available on-line or in print. See *APPENDIX L, Community Colleges Continuing Education* on page 167 for a list of community education programs.

In addition, many of the area's community and senior centers hold classes and special workshops on educational topics. See *APPENDIX P, Community and Senior Centers* on page 182. The seasonal lineups of local parks and recreation programs also offer educational programs and classes that may be of interest. See *APPENDIX L, Parks and Recreation Programs* on page 167 for a list of parks & recreation programs.

Museums and Historical Societies are another source of learning opportunities, especially for history buffs. Most museums offer a variety of programs to enrich understanding of the history behind their collections. See *APPENDIX M: MUSEUMS, HISTORICAL SITES, SOCIETIES* on page 168 for a descriptive list of history places to visit and volunteer for.

See *APPENDIX L: LEARNING LOCATIONS* on page 161 to start your search in these obvious, not-so obvious and easy-to-find places that offer a rich array of interesting topics.

Public Libraries: Learn, Volunteer, Friend

If you loved the feel and smell of old fabric and leather book covers, and were comforted by the creaks of uneven wood floors, you've got to see what's new

at today's libraries! You'll marvel at the sleek shelves, computer clusters, media centers, coffee shops, huge windows and meeting/learning rooms.

Far from becoming extinct, as some short-sighted prognosticators guessed, libraries have evolved into interconnected digital-age facilities. These virtual and community centers of learning have become inter-generational, multi-cultural gathering places, with 24-hour access via the internet to places far and wide.

Beyond housing book and media collections, library programs help kids learn to read, seniors find services and adults navigate computers. Libraries feature art shows and gardens and sculptures. They host cultural events, operate bookstores, provide computer and Wi-Fi, home delivery, conference rooms and community services. Multi-library city or county systems make it easy for patrons to borrow materials from any library in their system.

Learn and Volunteer

But one thing hasn't changed – libraries still make us feel good. Boomers still show up at libraries to learn, look up stuff and, yes, check out dear-to-our-

souls printed books. And, just maybe for convenience, download digital books.

Boomer library lovers also volunteer. Libraries need lots of volunteers – from teens to adults and seniors – who help throughout library operations. For example, they assist in computer labs, help put on public events and represent the library to the community. Inside, they shelve books, check in materials, assist patrons, perform office and administrative tasks, teach classes, work with books, help in after-school and summer programs and arts and crafts classes. Many are multi-lingual.

So libraries – like many cultural organizations – are not only places to feed your passion, but to give back to the community and to help others learn. In libraries you participate in one of your community's most important places for access to practical information, lifelong learning, resources and entertainment.

Friend Your Library

Library "Friends" groups support their libraries for charitable, literary and educational purposes. They help to raise money to support literacy projects as well as for day-to-day operations. They help build library collections, purchase equipment, work in bookstores and support activities such as summer reading programs. Another

plus for Boomers, Friends groups are just that – a place to make new friends.

See *APPENDIX L, Public Libraries by County* on page 163 to find libraries in your community.

CHAPTER 14: LEARNING OUT LOUD: TEACH-TALK-TUTOR-TRAIN

How would you finish this sentence?

I would love to use my knowledge of _____ to help people such as _____ learn about _____.

We each have acquired knowledge about and skills for something. We may have acquired it through school, work, a hobby, or people we hang with. Some things came naturally; others we've had to learn. So, is it now time to share that with others?

For example, you may know how to create a quilt or knit a hat, build a cedar strip canoe, play the guitar, write a short story or poem, play pinochle, tie a fly or kayak down a river. Can you cook a specialty dish? Or set up a chart of accounts, put up a website or use spreadsheet software? Maybe you're

passionate about some interesting aspect of history, a biography, an artist or a musician.

Think about it – if you're interested, others are too. Someone wants to know what you know. So why not help them learn? Find your own teach-talk-tutor-train niche and go for it! You know more than you think.

While we often use teaching, talking, tutoring, and training interchangeably, there are differences:

- TEACHING – Usually occurs in a formal group classroom setting, where you are the leader of a specific curriculum. A community college course on local history, for example.

- TALKING – Primarily from a platform before a group, where you are presenting as a keynote or workshop speaker. A civic, church or social group speech on healthy aging, for example.

- TUTORING – Happens one-on-one, where you coach and guide another individual to learn from you. Helping students improve their math skills, for example.

- TRAINING – Can be for an individual or group, where you are guiding their learning and mastery of a specific set of skills. Guiding people on how to use a computer software program, for example.

Discovering Your Niche Training in Three Steps

To figure out how best to position yourself, think about:

1. What is your passion and knowledge base?
2. Who wants to learn this knowledge?
3. Where can you reach those people and share what you know?

What to Teach?

What are you good at? What do you know a lot about? For what information do people come to you? What have you been invited to give presentations about?

Your past jobs and career are fertile discovery fields. What did you enjoy most? For what do you have special knowledge and expertise in your field?

Or do you have experience in a professional organization? For example, a special knowledge of technology, current industry trends, or research?

What about your hobbies or past hobbies? Do you build stuff? Make jewelry? Play cards, sew, knit, quilt, enjoy bird-watching? Take photos, build models? Seek out local adventures? Write stories or novels?

How about activities? What outdoorsy pursuits do you particularly enjoy and know about? Are you a special-interest gardener? A fisherman? Do you cycle, walk, hike, swim, play golf, tennis or pickleball? Would you love to help others learn?

Are there subjects you could tutor others on? For example, helping youth or adults with reading, math, science, writing, learning English, managing finances?

Who are Your Learners?

Next, think about the types of people who need the knowledge and experience you offer. What are their situations? How will you reach them?

Are they children, adults, seniors or some combination? Are you interested in one-on-one, smaller or larger groups? Narrow your choices down as much as possible.

Do you want to help people who are struggling with overcoming difficult life situations? Many social service organizations need people who came step in and serve in this way.

Where to Share?

Where is your best place to teach-talk-tutor-train? Do you need the structure of an educational institution, library or sponsor group? What learning situations would you prefer? Some may require formal education, others emphasize experience.

A multitude of teaching opportunities are found in traditional learning places – schools, universities and community colleges. Many Boomers share their expertise in the less formal community education programs and even get paid for it.

Library programs offer author programs, teach technical skills and language, and help young readers. Museums offer history learning. Community programs are more varied, with how-to programs on all varieties of hobbies, arts and crafts, health and fitness, and writing, to name a few.

Many schools and non-profits seek tutors to help children with reading, art, music and sports, as well as social skills.

Depending on your area of expertise, all types of community organizations seek speakers on topics of interest to their members. Their programs vary from current events to interesting aspects of community businesses, organizations, history and development.

See *APPENDIX O: TEACH-TALK-TUTOR-TRAIN PLACES* on page 173 for examples of organizations you can contact for opportunities to share your knowledge and expertise.

CHAPTER 15: LOCAL ADVENTURES: DAY TRIPPING

How often do we say, "I only visit the local sights when company comes to town!" Well, it may be time to venture out as a tourist in your own town. You'll find no better day-tripping paradise than Portland. We have it all – new

discoveries for everyone. Day trip solo, with friends, or find a group.

You needn't travel far to be in a forest, wetland, shipyard, river city, valley, beautiful garden, outdoor art collection, seasonal farmers market, art fair, history museum, local oddity, and on and on.

We offer big, medium, small and micro-towns. Lots of history and museums. Our communities blend shiny new urban with refurbished old and real old, still original and somewhere in between. While many places only can be reached by car, others are near to our expansive light-rail-streetcar-bus system. Venturing out, you'll find more than just our big trees growing taller. All kinds of businesses and organizations will happily show you around if you just ask. You'll find that just a little research – in your libraries, the local sections of bookstores, Chamber of Commerce offices, and visitor's centers –will bring you pleasant surprises as you explore your own back yard.

Places to Start

Here are some ideas to whet your local journey appetite and the tip of the iceberg when it comes to exploring your own town:

- Pick a cultural destination from the area's diverse collection of art galleries, museums and historical sites. See *APPENDIX B, Visual Arts Resources* on page 92 and *APPENDIX M: MUSEUMS, HISTORICAL SITES, SOCIETIES* on page 167.

- Enjoy the unique character, history and ambiance of small towns and communities. Walk about and visit local shops, bakeries, eateries, coffee shops and points of interest. Visit city, chamber of commerce or visitor center websites for maps and list of attractions and businesses.

- Take in scenery on river walks in places such as Milwaukee, Oregon City, Scappoose, Vancouver, West Lynn and Lake Oswego, or stroll along downtown Portland's East Bank Esplanade loop, or the south waterfront.

- Speaking of water, take a checklist tour of Portland bridges that cross the Willamette River. You'll have to cross the Tillicum – Portland's newest – on foot, bicycle, MAX light rail or bus. No cars allowed.

- Ride the MAX light rail to west-east end-points downtowns Hillsboro or Gresham. Walk to museums, theaters, and in Gresham, a Japanese Garden.

- Tour campuses of colleges such as University of Portland with wonderful surprises of art, architecture and sculpture. Other good strolling campuses are Laurelhurst (West Lynn), Pacific University adjoining the city of Forest Grove, Lewis and Clark College (Beaverton), Reed College (Portland).

- Take self-guided walking tours of area communities using free maps and descriptions available from walkoregon.com. These walking routes mapped out by Oregon Volkssport Organizations meander through downtowns, neighborhoods, parks and other points of interest.

- Catch the NW Portland Streetcar on NW 23St Street to loop to the South Waterfront and back for a visual lesson in Portland's architectural history.

- Put free local festivals such as the Forest Grove Chalk Art Festival on your watch list. For more ideas, see Public Art Walks and Festivals on page 93 or the events12.com/portland/ calendar of local events.

- Venture across the river south to north, if you're north, venture south. In Vancouver you'll find a friendly, walkable old-new downtown, local theater, river sights; drive further north to wetlands areas, botanical gardens, and plenty of Washington walking and hiking. From Washington, do the opposite to Portland.

- Tour small communities that dot the not-to-be-missed Columbia River Gorge. Drive down either side (Washington or Oregon) and return on the opposite. Take several trips to appreciate their unique character and hidden nooks and crannies.

- Drive through the produce and flower farms of Sauvie Island, enjoying seasonal ripening of pumpkins, fruits and vegetables, lavender and other flowers.

Group Day Trips

If organized group day outings appeal to you, visit the websites of organizations that offer inexpensive outings and trips. A variety of seasonal local trips are sponsored by local parks and recreation programs, community colleges and community centers. See their catalogs and classes schedule.

To find your next adventure see *APPENDIX L, Community Colleges Continuing Education* on page 167 and *Parks and Recreation Programs* on page 167, and *APPENDIX P, Community and Senior Centers* on page 182.

CHAPTER 16: MUSEUMS AND HISTORICAL SITES

Is history your passion? Do you love digging into the facts and stories of your community's, state's or county's past?

Maybe there's a particular facet of history that has captured your fascination – art, architecture, military, politics, transportation or home life, for example.

Or, could you take your passion deeper – dig into helping others appreciate history?

Museum exhibits in the Portland area include art, architecture, photography, film, rail transportation, maritime, science and industry, nature, forests and habitat, cultural museums and far more. Several history museums throughout Portland specialize in exhibits containing artifacts and stories of the state, city and local communities and neighborhoods. Many museums offer regular events, programs and tours to enhance the experience for their patrons.

Volunteering

Volunteers are the heart of most museums, large or small. Museums and historical sites offer a diverse assortment of roles to fit a volunteer's interests,

time, skills and experience. Whether you want to work with the public or in a behind-the-scenes role, there is something for you.

A great way to share your passion for history is by being a docent or speaker. As a docent – defined as anyone associated with volunteer educational services to a museum – you connect visitors to what they see, conducting tours or talking with groups.

If you are handy with and enjoy working with tools or machinery, museums can use your skills to build and take down exhibits, set up or drive machinery and equipment, or maintain interactive displays. Modelers help build miniature versions of displays. Museums often need assistant archivists who work museum collections to categorize, clean and store artifacts. Volunteers also may help research or transcribe oral histories.

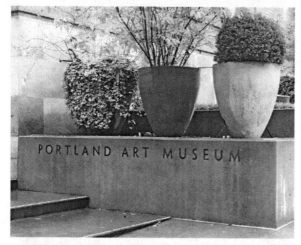

Volunteers are always needed to greet the public, work in museum stores, help with special events and tours, and perform administrative and fundraising tasks. Writers and editors, graphic artists, designers, and website designers support museum outreach, fundraising and marketing activities. They also serve on advisory and planning committees.

Museum and historical site volunteers receive tremendous personal satisfaction through discovering, preserving and sharing history. Many museums offer volunteer benefits such as memberships, discounts in museum stores, admission to special events, and recognition through group and individual events.

To get a feel for the volunteer activities with a specific museum, start with the museum's website. Those with volunteer programs will have a page detailing how to apply. That may require filling out a form and mailing or emailing it to the museum's volunteer coordinator. In some cases, you should contact the coordinator by phone. Background checks may be required.

See *APPENDIX M: MUSEUMS, HISTORICAL SITES, SOCIETIES* on page 168 for a descriptive list of history places to visit and volunteer for.

CHAPTER 17: ON THE WATER

If skimming the water in a kayak, canoe or dragon boat is your destiny, there are several areas to single or double paddle around in Portland. Here's a rundown of local options for great waterway wandering.

Places to Kayak and Canoe

Look closely off the Hawthorne Bridge downtown, and you'll spot kayakers year-round on the Willamette River, around Ross Island, the South Waterfront and near Willamette Park. Braver souls venture into the Columbia River in north Portland, not so intimidated by sharing the river with large cargo ships. The Columbia River Upper and Lower Sloughs offer more scenic above-water trips, with some natural obstacles and tides to deal with. Visit Columbia Slough (columbiaslough.org), Canoeing & Kayaking for more on the Columbia River.

To the northwest of Portland, the more serene Scappoose Bay channel, which feeds into the Columbia River, lets you get closer to nature and wildlife. The Clackamas River, southeast of Portland is considered one of the best rapid-water places in the state to kayak, but beginners are warned to not take it on without a guide.

In Washington, north of Vancouver, the Ridgefield National Wildlife Refuge offers paddling opportunities on the Columbia River, Lewis River, Bachelor Island, Lake River and Vancouver Lake.

If you want a family-friendly paddling place, try the Tualatin River.

Dragon Boating

Enthusiasts tell us that once you've tried it, there's no turning back.

In Portland, over-55 paddlers can join their own dragon boat club – Golden Dragons – for fun and fitness. They openly claim that old age and treachery will overcome youth and ambition. (You'll have to see for yourself, of course.)

Senior dragons complete against other dragon boats in Portland as well as in San Francisco and Victoria, B.C.

There are several ways to get into the long and skinny centipede-like boats skimming the Willamette River and Vancouver Lake for racing or just having

fun. The sport even has its own festival – Portland Dragon Boat Festival – in September. Or join a team in the Portland Rose Festival Dragon Boat Race which is held in June. Dragon boats are open to all ages and all abilities.

How to Get Started

You can get involved in paddling either on your own or in a group. Classes for all ages and abilities are conducted by area outfitters, city parks and recs, community colleges and other organizations. You also can check out the websites of a number of area

kayaking, canoeing and paddling clubs which provide lessons and sponsor events.

Clubs are another way to acquaint yourself with the rowing sports, and find kindred spirits. Whether you're a beginner or looking for white water adventure, there's a club here for you. Clubs always welcome newcomers and usually give you an opportunity to test the water before making the plunge.

See *APPENDIX N: ON THE WATER RESOURCES* on page 171 for listing of

places for equipment, lessons and tours, organizations and clubs, as well as fun and camaraderie for paddlers.

CHAPTER 18: POSITIVE CONNECTIONS, SOCIAL CLUBS, GROUPS

We are hard-wired to be socially active and engaged as a community. Research confirms what experience tells us – positive connections with family and friends make us healthier and happier and improve our lives. Without connections we become lonely, isolated and just a touch crabby!

We Boomers are no strangers to changes that upend our social lives. In fact, life-changing events such as retirement and loss of daily people contact, make us aware of our need and desire for new social activities. Many of us view retirement as THE opportunity to make new friends try out new things!

We find natural connections and community anywhere we gather around a common interest. Surrounding us are literally hundreds of places to meet and connect with others – places of worship, neighborhoods, colleges – and in classes and volunteer work, just for starters.

Portland offers Boomers unlimited options for social engagement. In fact, nearly everything in this book points to places where Boomers meet and connect with people around a common interest such as ...

Outdoor and Fitness Groups

A haven for outdoor and fitness enthusiasts, the Pacific Northwest gives rise to an abundance of outdoor groups. Outdoorsy types connect through a passion for their activity and being out in nature, as well as a liking for social gatherings. Most groups welcome newcomers; many offer activities at several ability levels; others hold year-round goings-on. Many also are Meetup groups. See *CHAPTER 19: THE GREAT OUTDOORS* on page 63, *CHAPTER 9: GARDENING: TEND A GARDEN* on page 35; *CHAPTER 4: CARE FOR ENVIRONMENT* on page 21 and *CHAPTER 11: HIKING AND WALKING: TAKE A HIKE!* on page 41, for more about outdoor groups.

Community, Adult and Senior Centers

Your local community and senior centers are gathering places specifically designed for social activity in convenient locations in all area communities. They encourage new and current members to take part in a wide variety of classes, workshops and social clubs. Activities include reading, dancing, card playing, arts and crafts, exercise and fitness, lunches and special dinners, computers and technology and seasonal day trips. See *APPENDIX P, Community and Senior Centers* on page 182 for a list of area centers.

Non-Profit Volunteering

Part of our social nature is a desire to make our communities better places to live, work and play. By volunteering we work side-by-side with others to help others – whether sorting donations at a food bank, helping kids read, shelving library books, serving on a city or county advisory committee, planting trees in a park, delivering flowers in a hospital – you get the idea. Learn more about volunteer paths in *CHAPTER 20: VOLUNTEERING* on page 65.

Parks and Recreation

Community parks and recreation programs offer places to connect and socialize with like-minded seniors and adults. These programs include classes in music, performance, writing and art, history studies, nature studies, books clubs, field trips and excursions, seasonal outdoor and fitness activities, and many other pursuits. They publish quarterly catalogs of activities on their websites. See *APPENDIX L, Parks and Recreation Programs* on page 167 for a list of area parks and recreation programs.

Community College Programs

Several community colleges offer programs on their academic schedules specifically for retired adults and seniors, or of interest to seniors, with emphasis on social learning activities. See *APPENDIX L, Community College Continuing Education* 167 for a list of area community colleges.

Hobby Groups

The common interest we find in hobbies naturally connects us. Many hobbies bring us together to work on projects, study more about our pastimes and socialize. A hobby is almost any aspect of anything that interests us – sports such as fishing or golf, arts and crafts, building something, collecting, reading, writing, studying history, cooking, DIY-ing – far more activities than we can list here. See *CHAPTER 12: HOBBIES: GET ONE* on page 45 and *APPENDIX K: HOBBY IDEAS FOR YOU!* on page 155 for more about Boomer hobbies.

Meetups

These are A-Z groups formed around a common interest or activity found on the Meetup.com website. Meetups run the gamut of interests – from commonplace to unusual and everything in between. Indoor-outdoor, travel-local, extreme-easy, social-introspective, culture-gritty, hobby-expert, open-private. Some are intergenerational; some specify age groups and some are totally Boomer focused. If you can imagine it, there is likely a Meetup for it.

Meetups usually are free or inexpensive to join, giving you the flexibility to try them out to see what fits. And if you're so inclined, you can start your own. Meetup.com makes it easy to find or start one. Go to Meetup.com and search by city, types of groups or name of activity.

CHAPTER 19: THE GREAT OUTDOORS

Maybe you've spent years chained to a desk, your eyes radar-locked on a computer spreadsheet and now, on the cusp of your next phase, it's time for a change of scenery!

You can morph from corporate beige to northwest green without a digital device. Experience tangible, touchable scenery. Photograph worthy landmarks. Go outside, away from all things electronic. Surround yourself with "now-that's-a-tree" firs, nature parks and rivers. Backdrop your tableau with northwest blue, or grey sky – even the rain has great beauty. Go to places where you can infuse fresh air into a foggy brain.

Portland's natural location means access to hundreds of forest and mountain trails, rivers, lakes, and out-of-the-way wetlands, watersheds, rivers and natural dramatic features beckoning to be explored. In old Portland, you can admire neighborhoods known for their architectural interest and walkability. Discover the abundant neighborhood parks right in your backyard. And don't forget the food carts, outdoor microbreweries and wineries. It's time to discover hidden nature gems within walking and driving distance.

Take it Outside!

You probably have a vision for next phase, but do you have a plan for living out your vision? Consider some important facts as you begin to map out your newly found free time...

- You're two hours from the coast; one hour to a mountain; less to wine country.

- In your own community, you are likely just minutes from a park or community gathering place.

- Portland is Outdoor Town USA. Outdoors is more a culture than a place here. Our culture goes beyond forests, the coast, and mountains. It's our community's commitment to parks, gardens, arts and cultural festivals, business areas, and community centers.

In your next phase plan, then, turn electronics to the "Not Now" mode and make regular appearances outdoors.

Think about what appeals to you, and start to explore some of these activities and get outdoors!

- **Cycling**. Grab your helmet and a map and pedal around cycling routes, trails, and clubs, events. See *CHAPTER 7: CYCLING: RIDE, BOOMERS, RIDE!* on page 29 for more about cycling in Portland.

- **Fitness Sports and Activities**. Places to get fit by walking, running, skiing, jogging, swimming, tennis and more. See more about the area's health and fitness options in *CHAPTER 8: FITNESS AND HEALTHY LIVING* on page 31.

- **Gardening**. Get the dirt on local gardening; how to enjoy, learn, socialize, and grow stuff in Portland area gardens. See *CHAPTER 9: GARDENING: TEND A GARDEN* on page 35 for more about all things garden in Portland.

- **Hiking and Walking**. Choose from hundreds of places to hike and walk, through neighborhoods, in forests, parks and cities, on mountain trails. See *CHAPTER 11: HIKING AND WALKING: TAKE A HIKE* on page 41.

- **Local Adventures**. Day trip to new outdoor experiences and adventures. See *CHAPTER 15: LOCAL ADVENTURES: DAY TRIPPING* on page 55 for ideas to get you started.

- **On the Water**. Explore the places and people of paddle sports in a kayak, canoe or dragon boat. See *CHAPTER 17: ON THE WATER* on page 59.

- **Outdoor Concerts, Farmers Markets, Art Shows and Festivals**. What better way to blend culture and outdoors in amazing Portland summers. See *APPENDIX B, Public Art Walks and Festivals* on page 93 and *Music Festivals* on page 82.

- **Outdoor Volunteering**.

Volunteer at parks, natural areas, wildlife refuges, trails, rivers, gardens and other outdoor places. See *CHAPTER 4: CARE FOR THE ENVIRONMENT* on page 21, *Chapter 9, Volunteer at a Public Garden* on page 36 and *APPENDIX H, Garden Friends Groups* on page 132.

CHAPTER 20: VOLUNTEERING

Portland's spirit of volunteerism reflects our love of life, nature, the environment and each other. And for those of us in the active Boomer

community, it's our time to give back to make our communities better places to live both now and in the future.

Boomers bring a lifetime of experience and skills that our communities need and value. We take our skills from paid jobs and invest ourselves in our communities. It's a win-win.

Volunteering tops many Boomer bucket lists, yet many are clueless about where to start. So where should you begin? With yourself, of course.

First, look at your skills and experience. Consider causes you feel passionate about. Or the opposite – what causes do you want to learn about? If you're looking for a cause to support, keep reading.

Next, find organizations with opportunities that match your skills, interests and passions. These are as varied and diverse as the fabric of the community. Believe it, they want you!

Here's how Boomers on the Loose™ in Portland can help.

- Browse through the *My Skills and Interests* questionnaire. Use it to focus on your natural skills, interests and passions, and types of work you'd like.

- Use the volunteer options list below to help you discover possible volunteer paths and lead you to some options.

Volunteer Paths

Look for a general category that interests you and the types of volunteers they typically need, then go to the reference pages for organizations you can research further or contact.

- **Animal Lovers.** Find your niche in organizations that rescue and care for dogs, cats and other small animals, horses, birds and other animals. Help care for animals, work in office or at outreach programs. Or get your pet certified as a therapy animal for friendly visits at places such as nursing homes and health care facilities. See *CHAPTER 1: ANIMAL LOVER OPPORTUNITIES* on page 9 and *APPENDIX A: ANIMAL RESCUE AND ADOPTION* on page 75.

- **Arts & Culture**. Behind-the-scenes volunteers in our diverse community of art and performance serve as docents and curators; design, build and maintain sets, sew costumes, usher, sell concessions, work in gift shops, or put teaching, writing, photography, website and office skills to work. See *CHAPTER 2: ARTS & CULTURE* on page 11 and *APPENDIX B: ARTS & CULTURE RESOURCES* on page 78.

- **City and County Government**. Opportunities at local government agencies include service on advisory boards, commissions and committees; helping at parks and recreation outdoor activities, farmers markets, city events and festivals; and assisting with various social services. See *CHAPTER 20, Government Volunteers* on page 69.

- **Community Service**. Volunteers give back to help the disabled, hungry and homeless, and people facing health and mental health challenges at many non-profit and faith-based organizations. Volunteers also work in outreach activities and behind-the-scenes administrative and technology areas. See *CHAPTER 6: COMMUNITY SERVICE* on page 27 and *APPENDIX E: COMMUNITY SERVICE ORGANIZATIONS* on page 106.

- **Healthcare**. Volunteers assist with patients in hospital, community health, mental health and hospice settings. They work for health-related causes they feel passionate about or have a natural connection to. They help with office and administrative tasks and community outreach programs and events. See *CHAPTER 10: HEALTH AND HEALING VOLUNTEERS* on page 39 and *APPENDIX I: HEALTH AND HEALING VOLUNTEER PLACES* on page 139.

- **Libraries**. More than books, today's libraries are gathering centers for learning and education with community classes and activities for all ages and interests. Volunteers assist with shelving, special projects, teaching, programs and events, maintaining media and much more. See *CHAPTER 13, Public Libraries: Learn, Volunteer, Friend* on page 48, *Libraries* on page 162 and *APPENDIX L, Public Libraries by County* on page 163.

- **Museums and Historical Sites**. Volunteers help preserve history and help others appreciate the past. You can work with a particular facet of history such as art, architecture, transportation, military, politics, or home life. Or the history of your community. Opportunities are endless. See *CHAPTER 16: MUSEUMS AND HISTORICAL SITES* on page 57 and *APPENDIX M: MUSEUMS, HISTORICAL SITES, SOCIETIES* on page 168.

- **Non-Profits**. At the heart of all non-profit organizations are volunteers who bring a wide variety of skills, interests and talents to serve their communities and keep their organizations running. For more see *CHAPTER 2: ARTS & CULTURE* on page 11; *CHAPTER 6: COMMUNITY SERVICE* on page 27; *CHAPTER 4: CARE FOR THE ENVIRONMENT* on page 21; *APPENDIX P, Volunteer Websites and Organizations* on page 183, or the volunteer pages of the websites of individual organizations.

- **Outdoor Volunteers**. Opportunities for the outdoorsy are plentiful in environmental organizations, friends-of-parks, parks and recreation activities and public gardens. Volunteers help restore parks, natural and wildlife areas, plant trees, shrubs and flowers as well as teach and guide groups. See *CHAPTER 4: CARE FOR THE ENVIRONMENT* on page 21; *APPENDIX D, Friend a Park or Natural Area* on page 98, *Protecting Ecological Areas* on page 101 and *Environmental Advocacy and Education Organizations* on page 103; *Chapter 9, Volunteer at a Public Garden* on page 36, and *APPENDIX H, Garden Friends Groups* on page 132.

- **Senior Assistance Organizations**. Pay-it-forward volunteers give back by serving in non-profits and other organizations that help seniors in daily living activities such as transportation, in-home assistance, grocery delivery and others. See *Senior Assistance Organizations* below and *APPENDIX P, Pay it Forward: Serving Older Adults* on page 179.

- **Senior Volunteer Places**. Several organizations are specifically built upon the life skills and experience that senior adults offer in areas such as teaching, training, management, accounting, working with youth, and many, many ways. See *Senior Volunteer Places* below and *APPENDIX P, Senior-Specific Volunteer Organizations and Resources* on page 178.

- **Volunteer Websites and Organizations**. Using websites that match organizations to volunteers, search for a gig that matches your location, interests, skills and availability. Choose from one-time or ongoing projects. Outside or inside. Long-term; short-term. Work with kids, adults or seniors. Many cities and counties also post volunteer openings for their departments as well as for their non-profit partners. See *APPENDIX P, Volunteer Websites and Organizations* on page 183.

Senior Volunteer Places

Options for Boomers looking to apply their life experience are non-profits that tap into the experience of seniors to carry out their mission. These programs recognize the valuable contribution of older adults to making a difference in our communities. Senior adults contribute valuable skills and experience in teaching, training, management and many, many other areas.

For example, senior volunteers in the AARP Experience Corps (aarp.org/experience-corps) work with children one-on-one and in groups to help kids in grades K-3 develop literacy skills and build self-confidence. Senior Advocates for Generational Equity (SAGE) (wearesage.org) inspires people over 50 to give of their time, talent and passion to enable younger and future generations to thrive. Senior counselors in SCORE Portland (portlandor.score.org) and SCORE Vancouver (scorevancouver.org) provide free business mentoring services to entrepreneurs.

See Senior-Specific Volunteer Organizations and Resources on page 178 for a descriptive list of organizations that are built around the life skills and experience that senior adults offer.

Senior Assistance Organizations

Senior assistance organizations are another way Boomers can give back. "I volunteer for organizations that help seniors because I'll need that help someday," say Boomer volunteers for senior-support organizations. "We provide a little help here and there that allows seniors to age in place."

Volunteers pay-it-forward through non-profits and other organizations that help seniors in daily living activities such as transportation, in-home assistance, grocery delivery and meals.

Senior Centers

Other places to help older adults are senior centers which give them a place to hang out, learn new hobbies, get fit and socialize. Located in communities throughout our area, senior centers provide a range of social services to help seniors live, learn, thrive, and socialize.

Senior centers also offer a variety of services including legal aid counseling, health education programs and activities, e.g. music, dancing, tai chi and yoga.

Senior centers need volunteers in a variety of roles.

- Teach classes in fitness, arts and crafts, writing, music
- Maintain libraries
- Cook and serve meals
- Technology and computers
- Trip leaders

See *APPENDIX P, Community and Senior Centers* list by county on page 182 to find one in your community and *APPENDIX P, Pay It Forward: Serving Older Adults* on page 179 for a descriptive list of non-profits and other organizations that serve older adults.

Government Volunteers

Do you enjoy an active interest in your local government? Many community-minded Boomers do and find that joining a county or city board, committee or commission is a rewarding experience.

Boards and commissions advise city and county agencies and bureaus on community issues and policies. They value the experience and the variety of expertise that retirees and seniors bring to the local governing process.

Counties and cities stress the importance of citizen advisors who represent the full range of diversity in their communities.

Volunteers can opt to serve on standing committees or citizen advisory groups that deal with specific issues. Websites of each county and city describe the functions and the makeup of their boards, committees and commissions. Many identify vacancies and how to apply.

Board members are generally appointed by a Board of Commissioners for a specific term. Members of city advisory groups are generally appointed by a mayor or the city council.

You can find many counties and cities that also have Committees for Citizen Involvement that focus on getting diverse groups of citizens active in government processes.

County Government

Citizen volunteers in county government take active roles in shaping policies, programs and decisions supporting specific county activities and goals.

Advisory boards and committees deal with areas such as aging, animal control, bicycles and pedestrian safety, budgets, clean water, historic preservation, parks, public health, arts, building codes, telecommunications, community action, tourism, traffic safety and more.

Each county also offers opportunities based on the unique features of its community. For example, the Clackamas County Hamlets and Villages committee encourages involvement from outlying unincorporated local communities. Washington County's Citizen Participation Organizations provide venues for citizens and decision-makers to learn about and discuss livability issues facing their communities. They include matters related to transportation, parks and trails, housing and business developments, public health, safety, emergency planning, schools and libraries.

For more information, visit the citizen involvement, boards or committee pages of your county website:

- Clackamas County (clackamas.us)
- Clark County (clark.wa.gov)
- Multnomah County (multco.us)
- Washington County (co.washington.or.us)

City Government

Citizen volunteers serve on boards and commissions like those of counties. Depending on the city, citizen committees support parks and recreation, budget and architectural review, libraries, arts and culture, tourism, citizen involvement, finance, water, zoning, transportation and utilities.

For more information, see the citizen involvement pages of your city's website:

- Beaverton (beavertonoregon.gov)
- Camas (ci.camas.wa.us)
- Forest Grove (forestgrove-or.gov)
- Gresham (greshamoregon.gov)
- Hillsboro (hillsboro-oregon.gov)
- Lake Oswego (ci.oswego.or.us)
- Oregon City (orcity.org)
- Portland (portlandoregon.gov)
- Tigard (tigard-or.gov)
- Tualatin (tualatinoregon.gov)
- Vancouver (cityofvancouver.us)
- Wilsonville (ci.wilsonville.or.us)

Law Enforcement Volunteers

Many communities need volunteers in special law enforcement programs. For example, Gresham Police volunteer members create a visible presence in the city's parks, trails and residential areas. In Hillsboro, volunteers participate in bike safety projects and community outreach crafts and games. Beaverton police volunteers help with car seat clinics, clerical duties, home security and similar programs. In Portland, the Reserve Officers program trains volunteers for uniformed, armed duties or non-uniform, unarmed duties. Police in other area cities need citizen volunteers for similar activities.

For more information, visit law enforcement or police department pages of your city's website:

- Beaverton (beavertonoregon.gov)
- Gresham (greshamoregon.gov)
- Hillsboro (hillsboro-oregon.gov)
- Portland (portlandoregon.gov)
- Tigard (tigard-or.gov)
- Vancouver (cityofvancouver.us)

VOLUNTEERING QUESTIONNAIRE: "MY SKILLS AND INTERESTS"

Answering the following questions will help you match up with meaningful volunteer activities. Use them to identify your skills, experience and passions. Identify the types of organizations that would absolutely welcome your involvement. You may want to get feedback from a spouse or friend.

There aren't any right or wrong answers, and you don't have to grade or score them!

1. What causes do you feel passionate about? You'll find supporters these throughout Portland.

   a) Caring for the environment: Clear air, clean water, sustainable forests, wetlands, watersheds, rivers, climate, parks, and lakes. Sustainable living, recycling and reuse.

   b) Caring for unserved or disadvantaged: Helping the hungry, homeless, disabled, elderly, disadvantaged families and youth, immigrants and refugees.

   c) Caring for animals: Rescue, adoption and care for cats, dogs, wildlife or other animals.

   d) Civic and municipal: support for libraries, law enforcement, municipal services and projects.

2. What types of places in the community attract your interest:

   a) Arts and Culture: Performing arts, theater, music, film, ballet, photography, art museums, historical museums, gardens, libraries. Most of these have supporting "friends of" groups or needs for event volunteers.

   b) Attractions in your community such as zoos, gardens, arboretums, museums.

   c) Educational institutions and schools of all types.

3. What organizations are you already connected with, such as faith-based organizations and schools that sponsor community or charitable programs? Could you help youth in a grandchild's school?

4. What types of professional organizations or unions do you belong to or that represent your professional background? They may be a source of causes or community programs.

5. What types of community events and festivals do you attend that you think would be an enjoyable volunteer activity? Portland is a haven for every imaginable type of festival. Would you enjoy working at your local farmers market?

6. Do you have a special connection with any of the numerous health conditions that would inspire you to volunteer for it? For example, organizations that address heart disease, cancer, childhood diseases, or disabilities?

7. Do you have a special place in your heart for people who are hungry, mentally ill, addicted or homeless?

8. What about medical centers and hospitals or hospice? Or community non-profit health clinics that bring healthcare to everyone?

9. Have you considered seniors programs, helping seniors not so fortunate who may be housebound? Or, the numerous senior and community centers throughout Portland?

10. What age group would you feel comfortable with? Infants, small children, teens, young adults, parents, seniors?

Next, think about the types of skills and experience, you can bring to an organization. Maybe it's just the plain old desire to work hard which so many organizations need. There are places for everyone. Are you a leader or a worker bee? Are you best in an organization's start-up phase, or doing its ongoing work? What would you be best at in an organization? Consider:

11. Do you have good people skills?

12. Do you like working with groups, or one-on-one?

13. Do you prefer working in the lead or in the background?

14. Can you do whatever is needed? Setup, take down, move things around?

15. Are you interested in technology? Computers? Phone systems?

16. What about administrative skills, typing, answering phones? Filing? Follow-up? Run an office?

17. Help teach musical, sports, or acting skills?

18. Do you have professional skills in areas such as medical, legal, fundraising, presentation, technology, that would benefit an organization or group?

19. What other considerations do you have? Transportation? Hours, physical limitations?

Once you've considered the types of organizations you're interested in and what you have to offer, it's time to put them together. See the reference pages for the activities and places that interest you:

- **Arts & Culture**. Visual and performing arts, museums, festivals. Look through *CHAPTER 2: ARTS & CULTURE* beginning on page 11 and *APPENDIX B: ARTS & CULTURE RESOURCES* beginning on page 78.

- **Caring for Animals**. Animal shelters and rescue. See *CHAPTER 1: ANIMAL LOVER OPPORTUNITIES* on page 9 and *APPENDIX A: ANIMAL RESCUE AND ADOPTION* on page 75.

- **Caring for the Environment.** Protection and preservation of outdoor habitats. See *CHAPTER 4: CARE FOR THE ENVIRONMENT* on page 21 and *APPENDIX D: CARE FOR THE ENVIRONMENT* (Resources) on page 98.

- **Caring for Communities.** Programs for emergency assistance, addictions, family and youth services; education; inclusion. See *CHAPTER 6: COMMUNITY SERVICE* on page 27 and *APPENDIX E: COMMUNITY SERVICE ORGANIZATIONS* on page 106.

- **Health-based conditions and organizations.** Associations based on health conditions, hospitals, medical centers, community health programs, hospice. See *CHAPTER 10: HEALTH AND HEALING VOLUNTEERS* on page 39 and *APPENDIX I: HEALTH AND HEALING VOLUNTEER PLACES* on page 139.

- **Libraries.** City and county libraries and library systems. See *CHAPTER 13, Public Libraries: Learn, Volunteer, Friend* on page 48, and *APPENDIX L, Public Libraries by County* on page 163.

- **Museums.** A wide variety of museums preserve histories of communities, industry, art, architecture, transportation and more. See *CHAPTER 16: Volunteering,* on page 57 and *APPENDIX M: MUSEUMS, HISTORICAL SITES, SOCIETIES* on page 168.

- **Outdoor Volunteers.** Participate in environmental preservation and protection (see *Caring for the Environment* above), and gardening activities. See *CHAPTER 9, Volunteer at a Public Garden* on page 36 and *APPENDIX H, Garden Friends Groups* on page 132.

- **Participating in Civic activities.** City or county-sponsored activities, justice and legal, law enforcement. See *CHAPTER 20, Government Volunteers* on page 69.

- **Senior Assistance.** Organizations that help seniors with day-to-day needs. See *CHAPTER 20, Senior Volunteer Places* on page 67.

Your responses are for you, to give you a good starting point for determining where and how you might best use your interests and abilities now that you are a Boomer on the Loose!

RESOURCE APPENDICES

The resources in this section include lists and descriptions of organizations such as those for volunteering, getting involved and others. While we make every attempt to include the most current information, changes to information may occur.

These lists were compiled from internet searches on the applicable topics and every attempt was made to be as complete as possible and represent an organization accurately. Many of the listings include descriptions that the author summarized for brevity from the organization's website content. The inclusion of all organizations in these listings is intended for information and reference purposes only; it does not represent a recommendation or endorsement of the organization for any purpose. Nor does it represent an organization's endorsement of this book.

If you notice anything that should be changed, please contact us at **BOTLPortland@gmail.com**

APPENDIX A: ANIMAL RESCUE AND ADOPTION

• Cats, Dogs and Other Pets • Birds • Horses • Zoos

The following are animal rescue and care organizations that welcome animal lover volunteers. Visit their websites for more information.

Cats, Dogs and Other Pets

- Animal Aid. Assists abused, homeless, injured and sick companion animals through rescue and adoption programs, financial and volunteer support of spay/neuter efforts in Washington County.

- Animal Rescue and Care Fund. Rescues, shelters and cares for homeless animals and places them in permanent homes. Portland.

- Animal Shelter Alliance of Portland. Metro-wide programs and services that reduce the number of homeless cats and dogs and save lives of all shelter pets that can be humanely and responsibly re-homed.

- Bonnie L. Hays Animal Shelter. Work with stray and abandoned animals. Every healthy unclaimed animal that comes to the shelter finds an adoptive home. Facebook. Hillsboro.

- CAT (Cat Adoption Team). Works with animal welfare organizations, animal control agencies, veterinary offices and other shelters to care for and re-home cats or kittens that otherwise face euthanasia. Sherwood.

- Cat's Cradle Rescue. Promotes well-being and adoptability; provides loving foster homes where shelter cats socialize while receiving medical care, spay and neuter surgery. Goal is adoption into qualified caring homes. Hillsboro.

- Clackamas Dogs Foundation. Promotes the health and well-being of dogs and people; supports educational and public service activities and programs. S.E.T. Team volunteers provide life-saving activities for dogs living in stressful environments.

- Core Paws. Core Paws is a non-profit website showcases hard-to-place homeless animals to help them find the perfect family.

- DoveLewis. Non-profit emergency animal hospital. Volunteers in non-medical areas such as animal transport, working at animal and fundraising events, community outreach.

- Family Dogs New Life Shelter. A no-kill dog shelter that rescues needy dogs of all breeds, ages and backgrounds. SE Portland.

- Fences for Fido. Builds free yard fences and insulates dog houses to improve lives of dogs living outdoors on the end of chains or tethers, or in small kennels. Spay/neuter services.

- Feral Cat Coalition of Oregon. Improves the welfare and reduces the population of feral and stray cats through spay/neuter programs and education.

- Friends Involved in Dog Outreach (FIDO). Improves the lives of animals; helps keep them out of the shelters and supports those in the shelter.

- Furry Friends. Small shelter providing services for re-homing cats including medical care, spaying and neutering, socializing and community education. Vancouver.

- House of Dreams. No-kill and free-roam shelter providing care for abandoned and homeless cats.

- Humane Society for Southwest Washington. Companion animal resources, reunites families with lost pets. Operates thrift stores. Vancouver.

- Indigo Rescue. Specialized, life-saving intervention for animals with characteristics and needs that render them unadoptable by shelter standards. Indigo Ranch in Vernonia.

- MultCoPets. Emergency response and rescue, investigations, animal nuisances, rehoming, helping with deceased animals.

- Must Love Dogs NW. Works to rehome dogs that are or will be homeless and those in shelter; educates on responsible ownership, behavior modification; training assistance.

- Northwest Animal Companions. Shelters and cares for stray, abandoned, neglected, lost, abused and/or unwanted animals until permanent loving homes can be found. Provides food, veterinary care, spaying or neutering, grooming and medications.

- Oregon Dog Rescue. No-kill shelter; dogs come from overcrowded local shelters, owners who cannot keep their dogs, and from high-kill shelters in California. Tualatin.

- Oregon Humane Society. Rescues, heals and adopts 11,000 pets each year; never places a time limit on how long cats, dogs and other pets stay. Pet Partners training program. Portland NE.

- Oregon Friends of Shelter Animals. Spay and neuter clinic, transports animals out of overcrowded shelters. Beaverton.

- POOCH. Re-homes shelter dogs that are cared for and trained by youth in corrections as a way to develop their personal and vocational skills.
- Portland Animal Welfare Team (PAW). Provides vet care to the pets of the homeless and low-income in times of crisis.
- Rabbit Advocates. Services, including foster and shelter care, and educational programs promoting welfare of domestic rabbits.
- Second Chance Companions. No-kill organization; 100% volunteer staffed. Feeds, cares for, adopts out, and spays and neuters as many animals as possible. Community education.
- The Pixie Project: Adoption and rescue center, offers pet adoption, pet owner education and support and low cost and free spay and neuter and veterinary services for homeless and low-income pet owners.

Birds

- NW Bird Rescue. Focuses on needs and welfare of orphaned exotic birds SW Washington and Portland. Offers Parrot adoption. Wild birds transported to Portland Audubon. Vancouver.

- Portland Audubon Society. bird rescue. Promotes the understanding, enjoyment, and protection of native birds, other wildlife, and their habitats.

Horses

- Horse Sense Riding School. Provides homes, training and jobs to horses at risk of auction or slaughter. Temporary foster homes and work for horses we hope to reunite with their families when they are ready. Care Team.
- Sound Equine Options. Cares for unwanted horses. Finds foster and adoptive homes. Volunteers involved in virtually all aspects of SEO, from cleaning stalls and fostering horses to finding the perfect forever homes. Gresham.

Zoos

Oregon Zoo. Volunteers (many are retirees) learn about, appreciate, and work with animals in a wide variety of ever-changing roles. You'll also have a choice of hands-on jobs, teaching or being part of behind-the-scenes zoo operations.

APPENDIX B: ARTS & CULTURE RESOURCES

- Literary Arts • Music Organizations • Performing Arts Theater Scene
- Performing Arts Companies and Venues • Visual Arts Resources
- Photographic Arts

Literary Arts

The following are lists of literary arts organizations that provide resources for readers, writers and authors of a wide variety of genres and interests. Visit their websites for more information.

Book Clubs, Groups and Readings

- Annie Bloom's Books. Neighborhood independent bookstore with regular readings and events.

- Book Club Meetups. A wide assortment of meetup groups throughout Portland for readers in a variety of genres from the classics to sci-fi, from traditional to weird and everything in between.

- Broadway Books. Locally owned, independent bookstore. Brings together authors and readers in an interactive environment and supports local authors.

- Friends of Mystery. Promotes educational study in all realms of "mystery" such as fiction, true crime, how mysteries are solved and other aspects; gives annual award for best mystery by a Pacific Northwest author.

- Friends of William Stafford. Non-profit, education-based organization that shares the work of William Stafford and furthers the spirit of his teaching.

- Literary Arts. Literary center which sponsors Portland Arts & Lectures, Oregon Book Awards & Fellowships for writers and independent publishers, creative writing workshops in public high schools, the Wordstock book festival and discussion groups around great literature.

- Library programs and events, including author lectures and discussion groups found at:
  - Beaverton City Library
  - Camas Regional Library
  - Clackamas County Library
  - Fort Vancouver Regional Library

- o Hillsboro Libraries
- o Multnomah County Libraries
- o Washington County Libraries
- NW Book Festival. A free outdoor book fair representing all genres; held annually in July.
- Oregon Poetry Association. An organization of poetry lovers who enjoy writing, sharing and learning about all forms of poetry through meetings, workshops and critique groups.
- Powell's City of Books. Portland's iconic independent bookstore. Sponsors a reading series featuring authors from all over the world several nights a week at several locations.
- Soapstone. Provides grants to support ad hoc events and short-term study that focus on the work of women writers. Events are free, study groups have a small fee; both open to the public.
- Wordstock. A Festival of readers and authors featuring author speakers, workshops and a book fair; held annually in November. Sponsored by Literary Arts.

Writing Organizations and Resources

- 9 Bridges. Meetup group. Offers positive, supportive critique groups that help improve writing skills; hosts workshops on craft and business of writing, partners with other organizations for member discounts and/or free admissions for events and services.
- Attic Institute. Writing center for independent writers. A private literary studio and a school for creativity. Offers workshops, individual consult groups and programs.
- Independent Publishing Resource Center. A place where local artists create and publish their own artwork, writing, zines, books, websites, comics and graphic novels. Provides artistic services through membership, use of the Center, workshops and outreach programs.
- Mountain Writers Series. Offers a variety of writing and reading workshops, classes and literary events by some of the region's finest writers and teachers.
- Oregon Poetry Association. Poetry lovers who enjoy writing, sharing and learning about all forms of poetry through meetings, workshops and critique groups.
- Oregon Writers Colony. Offers support to writers, from novices to published authors. Members benefit from classes, inspiration from teachers and colleagues, and access to Colonyhouse, a lovely writing retreat on the Oregon Coast.

- PDX Writers. Facilitates workshops and retreats for writers and offers a wide variety of prompt-driven workshops for new and seasoned writers.

- Portland Women Writers. Offers writing workshops that give women the opportunity to share stories in a fun, transformational and vibrant community; for and seasoned writers of all ages and backgrounds.

- Power of the Pen. Meetups to discuss projects - imagined, pending, in progress, successes! Networks with other writers in the Vancouver area to share best practices, techniques, motivation, helpful books and tools, and sessions focusing on technique or specific aspect of writing.

- The Guttery. An invitation-only critique group of writers dedicated to learning and sharing the art and craft of writing. Membership includes poets, memoirists, short story writers, and novelists who meet regularly to discuss the original work of two of their members.

- Willamette Writers. A regional organization of writers of all genres and at all stages of their careers who come to meetings, an annual conference and workshops to connect with their community, hone their craft, publish their work and advance their careers.

- Write Around Portland. Holds free writing workshops for adults and youth in hospitals, schools, treatment centers, correctional facilities, homeless shelters, low income housing residences and other social service agencies.

- Writing Meetups. A wide assortment of Meetup groups throughout the Portland for authors, writers, bloggers and poets of all interests and abilities, including critique groups.

- Writers Mill. Group of about 40 local writers of fiction, non-fiction, memoir, poetry, screenplays and songs. Holds regular meetings and talks with speakers, competitions and writing exercises; publishes journals.

Community Education and Parks and Rec Classes

Various writing programs and classes are offered through:

- Clackamas Community College (clackamas.edu)

- Clark College (ecd.clark.edu)

- Hillsboro Parks and Recreation (hillsboro-oregon.gov/departments/parks-recreation)

- Mt. Hood Community College (mhcc.edu)

- Portland Community College (pcc.edu/community)

- Portland Parks and Recreation (portlandoregon.gov/parks)

- Tualatin Valley Parks and Recreation (thprd.org)

Music Organizations

The following are lists of organizations that promote music, provide lessons, hold concerts and festivals, and provide other resources and opportunities for members and fans. Visit their websites for more information.

Bluegrass

- Taborgrass, weekly group lessons
- Oregon Bluegrass Association
- Washington Bluegrass Association

Folk Music

- Portland Folk Music Society
- Mandolin Concerts and Workshops

Classical Music

- Metropolitan Youth Symphony
- Oregon Pro Arte Chamber Orchestra
- Oregon Symphony Orchestra
- Pacific Crest Wind Symphony
- Portland Baroque Orchestra
- Portland Chamber Orchestra
- Portland Columbia Symphony Orchestra
- Portland Festival Symphony
- Portland Symphony Orchestra
- Portland Youth Philharmonic
- Rose City Youth Orchestras
- Vancouver Symphony Orchestra

Jazz

- PDX Dixieland Jazz Society
- PDXjazz
- Portland Jazz Orchestra
- Portland Youth Jazz Orchestra
- Portland Woodshed Jazz Orchestra

Music Festivals

- Cathedral Park Jazz Fest
- Chamber Music NW Summer Fest
- Improvisation Summit of Portland
- Jim Pepper Native Arts Festival
- Music Fest NW
- Northwest Strings Summit
- Oregon Music Festival
- Park Blocks Bluegrass Festival
- PDX Jazz Festival
- PDX Pop Now
- Pickathon
- Quiet Music Festival
- Vancouver Wine and Jazz Festival
- Waterfront Blues Fest
- What the Festival

Youth Music Education Volunteering

- Community Music Center. Provides opportunities for all ages to learn about, make and enjoy music through affordable music classes and low-cost concerts, workshops and instrument rentals. Program of Portland Parks & Recreation.

- Vibe of Portland: Offers affordable visual-arts and music classes to low-income neighborhoods through in-school, afterschool and studio classes and camps. Volunteers teach classes, help at workshops and put on shows.

- Ethos: Provides after-school music lessons, group classes, camps, multicultural performances and workshops to more than 7,000 students across Oregon each year. Volunteers assist with community events, office tasks, clean, repairing instruments, teaching, hanging posters and flyers, painting classrooms, repairs amps, electronics.

Vocal

- Aurora Chorus
- Portland Gay Men's Chorus
- Portland Symphonic Choir
- Pride of Portland Chorus

Performing Arts Theater Scene

The following describes types of theater you can choose from to participate in, attend, or work behind the scenes. See Performing Arts Companies and Venues on page 85 for a more extensive list of area theater venues. Visit their websites for more information.

Major Theatres

If you volunteer through Portland'5, you'll join a well-established volunteer organization that supports 5 centers – Arlene Schnitzer Concert Hall, Winningstad, Keller Auditorium, Newmark and Brunish venues. Its 500-700 volunteers, mostly retirees, donate hours as ushers, greeters, gift shop attendees, tour guides, reception desk attendants, office assistants and receptionists.

Portland Center Stage, the city's largest theater company, presents classical, contemporary and premiere works, holds a summer playwrights festival, and conducts education and community programs. Volunteers are ushers, Armory Ambassadors and office assistants, support casting, technical rehearsals and special events.

Volunteers at the Artists Repertory Theatre perform similar tasks.

Medium-Size and Regional Theatre

Medium-size professional and non-professional companies perform in area downtowns and suburbs. Volunteers usher, sell concessions and merchandise, help patrons, do hands-on behind-the-scenes tasks, sew costumes, build sets, and work in outreach. Examples of medium-size and regional theaters are:

- Broadway Rose Theatre Company, Tigard. Features Broadway-style musical theater and music reviews.

- Lakewood Theatre Company, Lake Oswego. Entertains with new productions and old favorites.

- Portland Playhouse. Performs original and popular plays and musicals.

- Profile Theatre. Focuses on works of a single Playwright for an entire season.

- Oregon Children's Theatre. Offers staged productions, outreach programs, and a children and teen acting academy.

Local and Independent Theatre

Dozens of smaller independent and home-grown performing groups are scattered throughout the area, entertaining in converted theaters, buildings, churches, and warehouses. Many are all-volunteer – from actors and directors to behind-the-scenes and office work. They include:

- Clackamas Repertory Theatre (Oregon City)
- Gresham Little Theatre (Gresham)
- Magenta Theatre (Vancouver)
- Theatre in the Grove (Forest Grove)
- Mask & Mirror (Tigard and Tualatin)
- New Century Players (Milwaukie)
- Sellwood Players
- Northwest Senior Theatre

Cultural and Social Statement

Several theaters portray stories from cultural or ethnic points of view. Many also are all-volunteer, from actors and directors to behind-the-scenes and office work. Examples are:

- Corrib Theatre. Stories filtered through the Irish experience.
- Jewish Theatre Collective. Performs great Jewish stories from the past and present.
- Milagro. Provides Latino focused theater.
- Passin Art Theatre. Performs from the African American perspective.
- Salt and Sage Productions. Explores issues from the female experience.

Experimental and Innovative

Ready for off-the-grid theater? Portland is a hotbed of innovative, in-their-own category groups. They need specialized skills on and off stage. Check their websites and call them.

- Do Jump's extremely physical theater blends theater, dance, aerial work, acrobatics visual and live music. Imago performances are known for characters and beings such as comedic amphibians, acrobatic larvae, circus boulders, and metamorphosing.
- Liminal creates immersive, media-rich environments that become elaborate worlds unto themselves.
- Shaking the Tree melds boundaries of theater and visual art with immersive theatrical experiences.

Performing Arts Companies and Venues

The following is a list of theater companies and venues in and around Portland. Visit their websites for more information on volunteering, auditions and schedules. While the intent is accuracy, be sure to check a theater's website for up-to-date information.

Alberta Rose Theatre	Renovated vintage mid-size theater housing acoustic music, art house films and live performances. Food, beverages. Portland NE.
Artists Repertory Theatre	Mid-size professional regional theater company. World-class acting, directing, design and stagecraft. Art in residence. Classes.
Back Fence PDX	Storytellers relate stories from true personal tales spun from a prompt, behind-the scenes stories combine with film, TV clips. Classes, coaching.
Badass Theatre Company	Diverse artists and audiences in new and inclusive stories. Expands boundaries of mainstream theater to reflect the many voices of our community.
Bag & Baggage	Professional theater, indoor and outdoor summer theater. Hillsboro.
Boom Arts	Presents, produces and develops socially relevant theater and performance.
Box of Clowns	Physical theater ensemble; clown troupe. Performs, conducts workshops.
Broadway Rose Theatre Company	Professionally produced Broadway musicals, comedies, and revues. Offers 6 mainstage, 2 children's musicals, teen workshop production. Equity and non-equity. Tigard.
Brody Theater	Entertainment and experiment. Actors from the Brody school, Saturday night Spontaneous Stage. Classes. Venue for Theatresports. Portland NW.
Clackamas Repertory Theatre	From farces to musicals to dramas, classics to world premieres. Produces familiar, yet brand new shows. Kids productions.
Clinton Street Theater	Small theater productions. Portland SE.

CoHo Productions	Small space theater. Co-production model of creating theater. Projects selected from submissions. Portland SE.
Corrib Theatre	Theatrical productions filtered through the Irish experience with a focus on contemporary and lesser-known voices. Portland SE.
Curious Comedy Theater	Comedy theater. Art of comedy. Classes.
defunkt theatre	Ensemble company dedicated to innovative productions that challenge conventional ideals of society and theater at a reasonable price. Portland SE.
Disjecta	Provides a catalytic platform for forward-thinking work by visual and performing artists. Collaborations between artists, curators, and viewers.
Do Jump	Extremely physical theater. Blend of theater, dance, aerial work, acrobatics, visuals, live music. Outreach programs.
Encore Senior Theatre	A theater group that enjoys entertaining and enriching the lives of area seniors, their families and friends coming together to experience live theater.
Experience Theatre Project	Bring educational theater programs to the underserved in Beaverton area by way of classes, kids summer camps and hands-on training.
Gresham Little Theater	Volunteer-based, provides entertainment and education, through various aspects of theatrical production. Year-round theater, dance, music and literary arts.
Hand2Mouth Theatre	Theatre ensemble committed to creating original work. Draws from dance, music, theater and design, blurring the line between performance and reality. Training and workshops. Youth theater.
Headwaters Theatre	Original multi-disciplinary artistic projects. Offers innovative, multidisciplinary and accessible artistic experiences and residencies along with integrative educational programming. Portland NE.

Hillsboro Artists' Regional Theatre (HART)	Dedicated to enriching the greater Hillsboro community by providing quality live performing arts at a reasonable price. Produces a regular season of creative, entertaining plays.
Hipbone Studio	Theater space events include drama, storytelling, dance, music, readings.
Imago Theatre	Defying classification, performances have included characters and beings such as comedic amphibians, acrobatic larvae, circus boulders and metamorphosing. Portland SE.
Journey Theater Arts Group	Professional-level youth and community theater classes. School year musicals throughout the area.
Lakewood Theatre Company	Regional professional non-profit theater. Actor training and development; presents plays and other entertainment. Lake Oswego.
Liminal	Experimental performance. Re-discovers 20th century avant-garde classic works, creates immersive, media-rich environments that become elaborate worlds. Portland NE.
Live On Stage	Artists, audience members and arts advocates dedicated to developing new opportunities for our amazing local talent. Portland SW.
Magenta Theater	Community theater in homegrown arts district of downtown Vancouver. All-volunteer cast and crew, local artists. Classes.
Mask & Mirror	Community theater in Tigard, Tualatin. Engage all interested in theater's many forms: artists, musicians, actors and directors.
Masque Alfresco	Produces classical and modern plays, summer park tours, staged readings of new plays. Training in classical and experimental styles of theater.
MediaRites	Tells stories of diverse cultures, gives voice to the unheard through arts, education, media projects. Mentoring, educational workshops and training.

Metropolitan Community Theatre Project	Produces main stage theatrical productions for Portland/Vancouver area.
Metropolitan Performing Arts Academy	Offers the community a complete well-rounded education in acting, singing, dance, musical theater, music and art. Adult classes. Vancouver.
Milagro	Latino theater, culture and arts education experiences.
New Century Players	Community theater, passionate volunteers bring professional-quality theater to Milwaukie/Oregon City area. Custom murder mysteries.
Nomadic Theatre Company	Entertains and educates through original, ensemble-based theater in theatrical forms including clown, mask, puppetry, dance, stilt-walking and acrobatics. School workshops and summer camps.
Northwest Children's Theater, School	Theater and classes for young audiences. Portland NW.
Northwest Classical Theatre Company	Classical theater co-production company. Camas, WA.
Northwest Dance Theatre	Pre-professional dance performances, community outreach and educational programs.
Northwest Senior Theatre	Light-hearted experienced (55 and older) performers who sing, dance, act, play music and love performing. Two annual musical variety shows.
Opera Theater Oregon	Group brings opera back into pop culture.
Oregon Children's Theatre	Theater and acting academy for children and teens. School trips and in-school programs, tours promote healthy living. Portland NE.
Oregon Repertory Theatre	Part of Portland'5 Center for the Arts. Collaborates with the region's finest, award-winning theatre artists.

Our Shoes Are Red / Performance Lab	Embraces live performance as a shared event; places art at center of intent. Emphasizes development, making work with scope, vigor, collaboration and innovative working techniques.
Pants-Off Productions	A radical queer creative production company that produces cabaret, live-music, dance and theatrical performances.
Passin Art Theater	Theater from the African American Perspective. Strives to pass art, history and culture from one generation to the next. Portland NE.
Pixie Dust Productions	Children's productions. All local creative and production teams.
Playwrights West	Original plays and premiers that provide thrilling, unique theater evenings, while exploring the complex, dynamic 21st Century human condition.
Polaris Dance Theatre	Contemporary dance company and dance center for youth, classes.
Portland'5 Centers for the Arts	Five theaters make up Portland'5 – Arlene Schnitzer Concert Hall, Keller Auditorium, and the Newmark, Winningstad and Brunish Theatres – vary in size, appeal and focus.
Portland Abbey Arts	Hosts art education classes, concerts community theater, cultural and social events.
Portland Actors Ensemble	Accessible classical theater in non-traditional environment. Presents Shakespeare in the Parks. Volunteers involved in graphic design photography, ushering, sew costumes.
Portland Area Theatre Alliance	Produces auditions, connects members with workshops; provides resources to theatrical community. Produces Fertile Ground Festival.
Portland Center Stage	Regional theater company, with classical, contemporary and premiere works summer playwrights festival; education and community programs.
Portland Experimental Theatre Ensemble	Contemporary performance; artist cooperative dedicated to creating new theatrical events that redefine the audience-artist relationship.

Portland Playhouse	Small, intimate performances stressing artist-audience interaction. Portland NE.
Portland Revels	Celebrates the seasons through song, dance, story and ritual of the past. A bit historical, classical and farcical. Portland SW.
Portland Shakespeare Project	Produces classical and contemporary works associated with classical material.
Portland Story Theater	Brings people together to hear real, true stories that ignite self-discovery and nourishes our capacity for empathy for ourselves and each other.
Portland Storytellers Guild	Storytelling theater where teller and listener recreate the stories of common humanity. Performances, workshops, classes. Story swaps.
Profile Theatre	Produces a season of plays by a single playwright to explore that writer's vision and influence on theater and the world.
Readers Theatre Repertory	One-act "small stories with big ideas at their heart," to amuse, confront, assuage and inspire. Intimate human relationships explore universal themes. Portland NW.
Reed College	Theater, music, dance and other performances and lectures open to the public. Events open to public.
Risk/Reward	New and experimental theater, dance, music and performance events as a vital cultural force in our community.
Sandy Actors Theatre	Offers live plays and entertainment year-round; workshops and mentoring.
Sellwood Players	Community theater group; performs at Sellwood Playhouse. Portland SE.
Shaking the Tree	Melds boundaries of theater and visual art by presenting audiences with thrilling and immersive theatrical experiences. Classes. Portland SE.
Siren Theater	Small Theater space. Home of Bad Reputation Productions. Kickstand Comedy.

Staged!	Staged! Produces stellar musical theater and nurtures the talents of young people. Classes. Outreach. We never put musicians in a pit. Portland SW.
Stumptown Stages	Musical theater for wide, diverse audiences; theater company in residence at Portland'5. Education programs. Outreach programs for underserved students.
Tears of Joy Theatre	Children's puppet theater celebrates diversity of world cultures. Teaches, enriches children, helps them create and perform with professional artists.
Theater in the Grove	Community Theater. Adult, children and teen programs. Forest Grove.
Theatresports	Public performance of a scored theater match between two teams that perform scenes in a certain category or genre. Brody Theatre. Portland NW.
The Liberators	Improv comedy troupe. Training center.
The Old Church	Performance and events venue in downtown Portland's west end cultural district.
Theatre Vertigo	Produces high-quality, ensemble driven theater; focuses on producing and developing new or rarely seen works. Shoebox Theater. Portland SE.
Third Rail Repertory Theatre	Brings to life exceptional stories that provoke dialogue, encourage empathy and inspire curiosity.
Portland Actors Conservatory	Provides rigorous actor training that engages the mind and heart of the artist, while cultivating a spirit of lifelong investment in the arts.
Triangle Productions!	A unique niche in the arts landscape producing rich stories told through diverse perspectives, particularly the gay perspective.
Twilight Theater Company	Community, all volunteer theater. Classes, workshops.

Visual Arts Resources

The following are lists of area art venues where you can engage in a variety of enriching and diverse art, film and photography experiences and volunteer opportunities. The lists include art museums, galleries, cultural centers, public art spaces and festivals. Visit their websites for more information.

Art Museums, Exhibits and Collections

- Portland Art Museum. World class museum with recognized permanent and ambitious special exhibitions, drawn from Museum holdings and the world's finest public and private collections.

- Museum of Contemporary Craft. Pacific Norwest College of Art. Documents the active role of both the Museum and the Pacific Northwest in the evolution of craft.

- Oregon College of Art and Craft. Hoffman Gallery. Showcases work by OCAC students, faculty, and regional, national, and international artists. Lectures open to the public.

- Portland Museum of Modern Art. Exhibits of national and international contemporary art.

Cultural Centers

- Lakewood Center for the Arts. Lake Oswego. Gallery of works that complement theater productions.

- Multnomah Arts Center. Portland. Gallery exhibits by local area artists. Seasonal art classes and workshops.

- Sherwood Center for the Arts. Gallery exhibits.

- Walters Cultural Art Center. Hillsboro. Gallery, art classes and workshops.

Public Art and Academic Galleries around Town

The following is a list of art collections in public indoor and outdoor spaces, academic institutions and other places. Visit their websites for information and locations of their collections.

- Art Institute of Portland Gallery

- Beaverton Public Art Program

- Clackamas Community College Alexander Gallery

- Disjecta Contemporary Art Center

- Doll Gardner Art Gallery. West Hills Unitarian Universalist Fellowship sanctuary.

- George Fox University. Roger and Mildred Minthorne and Donald H. Lindgren Galleries.

- Gresham Outdoor Public Art

- Hillsboro Public Art Gallery

- Lake Oswego Permanent Art Collection
- Kaiser Permanente Westside Medical Center
- Kathrin Cawein Gallery of Art. Pacific University
- Marylhurst University
- Oregon Convention Center
- Pacific Northwest College of Art

- p:ear Gallery
- Portland Community College Galleries
- Portland International Airport
- Portland Public Art Program
- Portland and Multnomah Public Art Search. Regional Arts Council
- Portland State University. College of Art & Design Galleries
- Portland Street Art
- Reed College, Cooley Art Gallery
- Tigard Public Art
- TriMet Public Art
- Tualatin Public Art
- Vancouver Public Art
- Urban Art Network

Public Art Walks and Festivals

The following is a list of area art walks and festivals which offer a casual, fresh-air way to stroll through art booths. Festivals always need volunteers with varied skills to help plan, promote, set up and take down festivals. Visit their websites for information.

- First Tuesday Art Walk. Downtown Hillsboro. Art galleries and Washington County Museum.
- First Thursday, Pearl District. Galleries stay open late.
- First Thursday, art walk Portland, Guide to participating galleries.
- First Friday, Portland, eastside. Galleries, boutiques, eateries promote arts.
- Last Thursday on Alberta. Showcases art, music and food. NE Portland.
- Tualatin ArtWalk. Self-guided downtown tour public art and natural and cultural history.
- SE Art ARTWalk. Artist in SE Portland. March.
- Tigard Art Walk. Art in downtown Tigard. May.

- Mt. Tabor Art Walk. Portland SE. May.
- Pioneer Family Festival. Oregon City. May.
- Lake Oswego Festival of the Arts. Outdoor exhibits, performances. June.
- Gresham Arts Festival. July.
- Tualatin ArtSplash Art Show. July.
- Alberta Street Fair. Local artists and crafts. August.
- Art in the Pearl. Art Festival, fine art booths. NW Portland, August.
- Oregon City Festival of the Arts. August.
- Art in the Pearl. September.
- Time-Based Art Festival. September.
- Chalk Art Festival and Annual Corn Roast. Downtown Forest Grove. September.
- Beaverton Arts Mix. Art Show. October.
- Wine Walk. Art and wine in Lake Oswego. October.
- Wild Arts Festival. Nature in Art. November.
- Wilsonville Festival of Arts. November.

Art Commissions and Alliances

The following is a list of area cultural organizations and city and county commissions that welcome participation in planning and overseeing community art projects. They promote the growth of arts and culture in their communities through public art projects, grants, advocacy, special events and participation on arts boards, committees and commissions. Visit their websites for information.

- Arts Council of Lake Oswego
- Arts of Clark County
- Beaverton Arts Commission
- Clackamas County Arts Alliance
- Clark County Arts Commission
- Cultural Coalition of Washington County
- Gresham Art Committee
- Hillsboro Arts and Culture Council
- Forest Grove Public Arts Commission
- Milwaukee Arts Committee
- Oregon City Arts Commission
- Regional Arts and Cultural Council

- Sherwood Cultural Arts Commission
- Tualatin Arts Advisory Committee
- Westside Cultural Alliance
- Wilsonville Arts & Culture Council

More Volunteer Opportunities in Art

The following is a list of organizations that offer opportunities to volunteer in youth art programs. Visit their websites for more information.

- CHAP (Children's Healing Art Project). Teaching artists lead art adventures for children and their families at several area hospitals. Volunteers help with art projects, mailings and events.
- p:ear. Serves homeless and transitional youth through education, art and recreation. Volunteers assist at artistic workshops; host and guide tours for gallery exhibitions.
- PHAME Academy. Inspires individuals with developmental disabilities to lead full, creative lives through arts education and performance. Integrates students into artistic mainstream of visual arts, creative writing, acting, music, dance and theater.
- Young Audiences Arts for Learning. Inspires young people to expand their learning through the arts. Volunteers assist teaching artists and work in office and at events.
- The Giving Tree NW. Provides art programs that engage vulnerable populations in art and other activities. Volunteers involved in variety of art and other roles.
- Vibe of Portland. Artists teach visual-arts and music classes to low-income children through in-school, afterschool and studio classes and camps. Volunteers teach, help at workshops and put on shows.

Film Organizations and Resources

- Meetup Groups. Portland is home to a number of Meetup groups, clubs and discussion groups of people who love to view and make films. Interests range from silent, art, horror and sci-fi films, to film-making and critique groups, indie film-making and more.
- Northwest Film Center. A centerpiece in Portland's film scene associated with the Portland Art Museum. Offers a variety of film and video exhibition, education and information programs, and festivals primarily directed to the residents of the Pacific Northwest.
- Willamette Writers. Writing organization that provides screenwriting and film-making curriculum for film and television arts.
- Women in Film Portland. Women's film organization focusing on education, outreach and professional development.

Film Festivals

- NW Film Center: Reel Music (January); International Film Festival (February); Portland Jewish Film Festival (June); Top Down: Rooftop Cinema (July-August); Northwest Filmmakers' Festival (November); Fresh Film Northwest (November); Japanese Current (December).

- African Film Festival. Portland Community College. February.

- Bike Film Festival. Bicycling films. May.

- Through Indian Eyes. Native American films. May.

- Portland Horror Film Festival. Independent horror films. June.

- Portland Film Festival. Conference and film festival. August/September.

- Oregon Independent Film Festival. September.

Photographic Arts

Photo Galleries

- Blue Sky Gallery. Exhibits work of emerging and established artists. Volunteers prepare and install exhibitions, support administrative staff, and greet visitors at receptions.

- New Space Center for Photography. Nonprofit resource center and community hub for students, working artists, professional photographers, educators and photo-enthusiasts of all types. Classes, photo lab resources.

- Portland Art Museum. Rotating exhibits from the museum's permanent collection in the Jubitz Center for Modern and Contemporary Art.

- Portland Fire and Rescue Vintage Photo Galleries. Photo galleries of fire stations in historical sections of Portland.

Photography Clubs and Resources

- Portland Camera Club

- Portland Photo Forum

- Orenco Photo Club

- Meetups. Photography meetups in Portland.

- Photography Classes. Offered through community education programs at:
  - Clackamas Community College (clackamas.edu)
  - Clark College (ecd.clark.edu)
  - Hillsboro Parks and Recreation (hillsboro-oregon.gov)
  - Mt. Hood Community College (mhcc.edu)
  - Portland Community College (pcc.edu)
  - Portland Parks & Recreation (portlandoregon.gov)

APPENDIX C: BUSINESS STARTUP RESOURCES

The following are lists of city economic development and chamber of commerce organizations that provide resources for new and existing businesses. Visit their websites for more information.

- Beaverton Economic Development. Web page of resources for existing and start-up businesses including a Start a Business page of resources.

- Business Oregon. Oregon's economic development agency. Provides a variety of resources to help entrepreneurs start and finance a business.

- Hillsboro Chamber of Commerce. Provides Business Resources Center counseling and online resources.

- Portland Business Alliance. Greater Portland's Chamber of Commerce. Free Small Business Advising service.

- Prosper Portland. Portland's economic and urban development agency. Sponsors economic development programs that support small business, improve access to workforce training and create jobs.

- Portland Economic Development. Studies and information about the city's economic sectors.

- Vancouver Economic Development. Provides information on business workshops, networking and training activities through Vancouver Business Resources page.

- Vancouver Small Business Assistance Program. Chamber of Resource Center. Business counseling for startups and existing businesses in Vancouver.

Various other community organizations also provide resources to the business community. Visit their websites for more information.

- City of Forest Grove Economic Development
- City of Hillsboro Economic Development
- Forest Grove/Cornelius Chamber of Commerce New Business Resources
- Gresham Chamber of Commerce Business Resources
- Hillsboro Chamber of Commerce Resource Center
- Lake Oswego Business
- Tigard Chamber of Commerce Business Resources
- Tualatin Chamber of Commerce Economic Development

APPENDIX D: CARE FOR THE ENVIRONMENT

- Friend a Park or Natural Area • Protecting Ecological Areas
- Environmental Advocacy and Education Organizations

If you're passionate about sustaining and protecting our amazing environment, look at the lists below to find your ideal volunteer activity. Visit their websites for more information.

Friend a Park or Natural Area

The following is a list of parks and natural areas with Friends and volunteer groups in your county.

Clackamas County

- Lake Oswego Parks & Recreation Friends Groups. Friends and neighborhood groups doing stewardship activities in parks and natural areas. Groups and individuals plant native species, clear invasive species, and other projects.

- North Clackamas Parks & Recreation. Work parties plant, clean trails, pull ivy.

- Oregon City Parks & Recreation. Seasonal volunteer activities. Volunteers are park hosts.

Clark County

- Clark County Parks Volunteer Program. Outdoor volunteers and work parties tackle clean-up, invasive plant removal, garden maintenance, trail maintenance. Green visitors.

- Clark County Adopt-A-Park Program. Ongoing opportunity to help beautify a park, enhance safety, and build community.

- Friends of the Ridgefield National Wildlife Refuge. Cultural education, hiking, tour guiding, conservation, visitor services, habitat restoration.

- Vancouver Parks Volunteer Programs. Adopt-a-park, work parties, ivy pull, park maintenance, cleanup.

Multnomah County, Gresham, East

- City of Gresham. Natural resources volunteers do bird surveys, replant natural areas, build habitat structures, remove weeds.

- Columbia River Gorge, Friends. Works to protect the scenic, natural, cultural, and recreational resources of the Columbia River Gorge. Work parties, lead hikes, outings.

Multnomah County, Portland Parks & Recreation (PP&R)

- PP&R and volunteer partners and friends groups, help steward, advise and support parks, natural areas, and other programs. See list of PP&R partners and contacts on website.

- Community Gardens Volunteers. PP&R work parties in Portland to spruce up community gardens – weeding, mulching, pruning, building beds, laying paths.

- Friends of Natural Areas. Lists and contacts of volunteers, neighbors, co-workers and park lovers who do hands-on restoration with support of PP&R staff. Natural areas included in this program are:

  o Arbor Lodge Park
  o Friends of Tideman Johnson
  o Forest Park-No Ivy League
  o Friends of Errol Heights
  o Friends of Hoyt Arboretum
  o Friends of Marquam Nature Park
  o Friends of Mt. Tabor Park Weed Warriors
  o Friends of Powell Butte
  o Friends of Ross Island Natural Area
  o Friends of Terwilliger & West Willamette Restoration Partnership
  o Friends of Woods Park
  o Laurelhurst Park
  o Lents Springwater Habitat Restoration South Portland Riverbank Partners

Multnomah County, Portland, N, NE

- Friends of Peninsula Park Rose Garden

Multnomah County, Portland NW

- Forest Park Conservancy. Fosters ecological health of the urban wilderness park, maintains extensive trails network. Work parties to remove invasive plants, fix trails, plant and prune.

Multnomah County, Portland SE

- Friends of Laurelhurst. Helps keep Laurelhurst Park functioning well and looking vibrant.

- Friends of Mt. Tabor Park. Stewards of the 197-acre unique volcanic park space.

- Friends of Powell Butte. Park neighbors and friends work with PP&R in planning and implementing park improvements.

Multnomah County, Portland SW

- Friends of Marquam Nature Park. Works with PP&R on preservation and education activities.
- Friends of Terwilliger. Community work parties to remove invasive plants in this unique linear park.
- Friends of Tryon Creek State Park. Stewardship and restoration, environmental education.
- Hoyt Arboretum Friends. A membership-based, nonprofit partnering with Portland Parks and Recreation to support Hoyt Arboretum. Maintains plant and tree collections, hiking trails.
- World Forestry Center. Informs, educates, and informs people about the world's forests and trees, and environmental sustainability. Organizations and business groups volunteers.

Washington County

- City of Tualatin. TEAM Tualatin, works with park crews to water and mulch plants, plan gardens, take care of parks.
- Forest Grove Parks & Recreation. Volunteer at Parks. Volunteer through Adopt-a-Park program. Weeding, planting flowers, spreading bark dust, clean up, invasive plants.
- Friends of Tualatin River National Wildlife Refuge. Environmental education, greet trail guests; interpretative programs, help at annual Bird Festival, nature camps. Sherwood.
- Friends of Wapato Lake National Wildlife Refuge. Habitat improvement work parties, volunteer naturalist. US Fish and Wildlife. Sherwood.
- Hillsboro Park Projects. Park beautification and habitat enhancement projects through Grassroots Hillsboro, Clean up flower beds, plant trees, and shrubs, built fences, remove invasive species. Trail grooming.
- Hillsboro Parks & Recreation Adopt a Park. Adopt-a-Park. Local groups, families, and businesses get involved and help keep parks safe and clean.
- Jackson Bottoms Wetlands Preserve. Outdoor crews, education center guides, outreach, monitor water quality, special projects.
- The Wetlands Conservancy. Sponsors volunteer wetlands restoration events in area wetlands. Hedges Creek, Tualatin wetlands.
- Tualatin Hills Park & Recreation District. Nature volunteers. Adopt-a-Park, friends groups, nature education, park improvement, environmental education and wildlife habitat enhancement.
- Tualatin Hills Friends Groups. Work with park staff to help restore nature area parks and provide educational programs; provide watershed stewardship.

- o Friends of Tualatin Hills Nature Park
- o Friends of Fanno Creek
- o Friends of Beaverton Creek
- o Tualatin River Watershed Council

Protecting Ecological Areas

The following is a list of groups dedicated to maintaining ecological areas.
Visit their websites for more information.

- Columbia Riverkeepers.
Works within communities to
restore and protect the water
quality of Columbia River and
all life connected to it, from
headwaters to the Pacific
Ocean. Volunteers: Monitor
water quality, educate
communities, lead field trips.

- Columbia Slough Watershed
Council. A diverse group of
neighbors, property owners,
businesses, environmental
groups, recreation advocates,
and government agencies who work to restore and enhance the 60 miles
of waterways, wetlands, and slow moving channels in the slough.
Volunteers: Plant, mulch, remove invasive plants, clean litter.

- Forest Park Conservancy. Protects and fosters the ecological health of
Forest Park, maintains and enhances the park's extensive trails network,
and inspires community appreciation and stewardship of the iconic, urban
wilderness as a gift for future generations. Volunteers: Maintain trails and
enhance habitat.

- Friends of the Columbia Gorge. Protects the scenic, natural, cultural and
recreational resources of the Columbia River Gorge. Volunteers:
Stewardship work parties, lead hikes or outings, supervise information
tables, participate in hearing, rally or phone bank.

- Friends of Ridgefield (WA) National Wildlife Refuge. Promotes educational
programs of the Ridgefield NWR, and works to protect and enhance its
wildlife habitat. Volunteers: Nature education, wildlife habitat restoration,
and naturalist corps.

- Friends of Terwilliger. Protects the natural character and scenic beauty of
the Terwilliger Parkway corridor. Habitat and watershed restoration
along the parkway. Volunteers: Restoration work parties and advocacy.

- Friends of Trees. Brings people together to plant and care for city trees and green spaces in Pacific Northwest communities. Volunteers: Various group and individual planting, loading, weekends, weekdays.

- Jackson Bottoms Wetlands Preserve. Outdoor crews, education center guides, outreach, monitor water quality, special projects. Hillsboro.

- Lower Columbia Estuary Partnership. A partnership advancing science, protecting ecosystems, and building connections to sustain the lower Columbia River estuary. Volunteers: Tree planting events, and other clean-up and restoration; some involve canoeing and kayaking.

- Metro. A regional governing body that manages 17,000 acres of parkland for recreation. Volunteers: work in some of the region's newest natural areas working with park gardens, native plants, seeds, restoration, trail counts at various locations.

- Nature Conservancy (Oregon). International organization with local activities, works to conserve the lands and waters on which all life depends. Volunteers: Family friendly work parties maintain hiking trails, restore natural areas, plant native plants, clean up areas.

- Nature Conservancy (Washington). International organization works to conserve the lands and waters on which all life depends. Volunteers: Help with a variety of projects from planting trees to answering phones, and a whole lot in between.

- Oregon Wild. Works to advocate for and protect and preserve Oregon's wildlands, wildlife and waters. Hikes and events. Take Action: Outdoor writing, recreation, office tasks, phoning, board of directors, on-ground activities in wild areas. Hike leaders, map landscapes, activism, help in office and at events.

- Oswego Lake Watershed Council. Works to improve the condition and health of the Oswego Lake watershed and its stream network. Volunteers and Friends Groups: Restoration planting and invasive plant removal; education events.

- Ridgefield (WA) National Wildlife Refuge. Provides habitat for wintering waterfowl. Invites people of all abilities to experience nature and share outdoor traditions. Volunteers: Restore habitat, conduct wildlife surveys, teach cultural, environmental education and greet public.

- Shillpoo Wildlife Area. 2,370-acre wildlife area, located within the floodplain of the Columbia River in Clark County. Volunteer through Washington Department of Fish and Wildlife.

- Smith & Bybee Wetlands Natural Area. 205-acre waterway and haven for many animal species, and heaven for nature-seeking hikers, bikers and kayakers. Contact Metro for current volunteer opportunities.

- Steigerwald Lake. Stunning views and year-round wildlife viewing opportunities, managed by National Fish and Wildlife Services. Volunteers: Restore habitat. Teach others about wildlife resources. On- and off-site restoration, education and outreach. Vancouver.

- Tualatin River National Wildlife Refuge. Urban wildlife refuge managed to mimic the natural seasonal cycle, so whatever the season, you'll see many kinds of wildlife here. Get Involved: Participate in restoration and education. Sherwood.

- The Wetlands Conservancy. Dedicated to conserve and promote wetlands to support fish and wildlife, clean water, open space, public safety, and appreciation of nature. Volunteers: Wetlands restoration tasks such as monitor beaver dams, plant native plants, remove invasive plants.

- Trailkeepers of Oregon. Maintenance and stewardship projects that preserve existing trails. Committed to restoring proper funding and renewing public agency interest in trails. Provides on-line *Oregon Hikers Field Guide*. Get Involved: Hiking and trail advocates, outreach, trail work, communicating news, education.

- Tryon Creek Watershed Council. Restores, protects, and enhances the ecological health and function of unique urban watershed. Volunteers: Restoration, cleanup, replant stream banks, remove invasive plants, lead teams, outreach and school education programs. Portland SW.

- Tualatin Riverkeepers. Dedicated to holistic watershed management for Tualatin River and its 27 creeks for community benefit. Volunteers: Participate in watershed watch, as field trip or day camp leaders, in restoration plantings, and event helpers.

- Vancouver Watersheds Alliance. Works with City to provide community outreach, environmental restoration, promote volunteerism, and care for water resources. Volunteers: Families, individuals, college students and school groups; stewardship, outreach and office.

- Wapata Lake. National Wildlife Refuge designated to protect and restore habitats for benefits of fish, wildlife and people. Not yet open to the public. Get Involved: Restoration work parties, volunteer naturalists. Sherwood.

- Willamette Riverkeepers. Works to protect and restore the Willamette River. Volunteers: Restoration tasks, paddle trip assistant, help at outreach events, monitor water quality; provide feedback.

Environmental Advocacy and Education Organizations

The following is a list of environmental advocacy and education organizations. Visit their websites for more information.

- Cascadia Wild. Inspires personal connection to nature and community; holds classes, events.

- Center for Diversity & the Environment. Harnesses the power of racial and ethnic diversity to transform the U.S. environmental movement by developing leaders, catalyzing change within institutions and building alliances.

- Columbia Springs. 100-acre urban natural area. Offers K-12 field trips, community events, summer camps and sustainability workshops, trout hatchery. Volunteers: Help with field trips, stewardship projects, community events, weeding gardens. Vancouver.

- Friends of Outdoor School. Introduces children to nature, ecology, the environment, natural resources and animal and plant life. Volunteers: Special needs on-on-one, student leaders, classroom speakers, teacher trainers, office, outreach and marketing.

- Friends of the Columbia Gorge. Protects the scenic, natural, cultural and recreational resources of the Columbia River Gorge. Volunteers: Stewardship work parties, lead hikes or outings, supervise information tables, participate in hearing, rally or phone bank.

- Friends of Terwilliger. Protects the natural character and scenic beauty of the Terwilliger Parkway corridor. Habitat and watershed restoration along the parkway. Volunteers: Restoration work parties and advocacy.

- Northwest Earth Institute. Builds communities of change to address environmental conservation. Volunteers: Mentor new groups, develop and update curriculum, help in office and at community events.

- Oregon Environmental Council. Works for clean air and water, healthy climate, unpolluted landscapes and sustainable food and farms. Volunteers: Policy research, engage community, fundraising, marketing.

- Oregon Sierra Club. Promotes conservation of Oregon's natural environment by influencing public policy decisions – legislative, administrative, legal and electoral. Members and volunteers: Lead outings, analyze Environmental Impact Statements, create displays, greet guests at events, testify at hearings, mail alerts, speak to kids, call legislators.

- Oregon Wild. Works to protect and preserve Oregon's wildlands, wildlife and waters. Hikes and events. Volunteers: Outdoor writing, photography, community events, activism.

- Portland Parks Foundation. Brings resources for the long-term stewardship of Portland's parks and park programs, and ensures that they remain publicly supported. Volunteers: Attend and speak up at public meetings, blog about parks, submit photos.

- Rewild Portland. Educates public on earth-based arts, traditions and technologies at workshops, programs and community-building. Volunteers: Teach, facilitate classes, assist at Free Skill Services, outreach.

- The Wetlands Conservancy. Dedicated to conserving and promoting wetlands to support fish and wildlife, clean water, open space, public safety and appreciation of nature. Volunteers: Restore wetlands, monitor beaver dams, plant native plants, remove invasive plants.

- Trailkeepers of Oregon. Maintenance and stewardship projects to preserve existing trails to avoid trail neglect. Committed to restoring proper funding and renewing public agency interest in trails. Provides on-line *Oregon Hikers Field Guide*. Volunteers: Hiking and trail advocates, outreach, trail work, communicating news, education.

- Tryon Creek Watershed Council. Restores, protects, and enhances the ecological health and function of unique urban watershed. Volunteers: Restoration, cleanup, replant stream banks, remove invasive plants, lead teams, outreach and school education programs.

- Tualatin Riverkeepers. Dedicated to holistic watershed management for Tualatin River and its 27 creeks for community benefit. Volunteers: Participate in watershed watch, as field trip or day camp leaders, in restoration plantings; event helpers.

- Vancouver Watersheds Alliance. Works with City on community outreach, environmental restoration, promoting volunteerism and caring for water resources. Volunteers: Families, individuals, college students and school groups; stewardship, outreach and office.

- Washington Sierra Club. Involved in environmental education, conservation, and political issues to protect air, land and water. Volunteers: Education, outings, website, fundraising, administrative work.

- Willamette Riverkeepers. Works to protect and restore the Willamette River. Volunteer: Restoration tasks, paddle trip assistants, help at outreach events, monitor water quality; provide feedback.

- World Salmon Council. Provide experiential education and encounters with Pacific wild salmon to connect students and adults with nature and empower community engagement. Engages students in Salmon Watch program. Volunteers: Teachers.

APPENDIX E: COMMUNITY SERVICE ORGANIZATIONS

• Addictions and Mental Health • Disability Services • Emergency Services • Family and Social Services • Food Banks and Gardens • Hunger and Homeless Services • Youth Programs

The following are lists for various types of community services organizations. Visit their websites for more information about volunteering.

Addictions and Mental Health

The following is a list of area mental health programs. Programs may require background checks of volunteers. Visit their websites for more information.

- ASHA International. Promotes personal, organizational, and community wellness through mental health education, training and support. Volunteers are involved in marketing and PR, development, fundraising, grant writing, photography, social media, health and wellness.

- Baby Blues Connection. Supports women and families coping with pregnancy and postpartum mood disorders, and professionals who serve them. Volunteers provide mom-to-mom, dad, phone, mentor and email support, as well as office and social media.

- Circles of Support & Accountability. Programs to heal individuals and a community after violent crime.

- Comprehensive Options for Drug Abusers. Treats people with alcohol, drug and mental health challenges. Volunteers paint CODA residences, plant gardens, make afghans, host barbecues, even organize closets, hold fundraising events.

- De Paul Treatment Centers. Chemical dependency treatment services to men, women, youth and families. Volunteers provide peer support.

- Good News Community Health Center. Faith- and community-based health center offers primary care, diabetes education, foot care and mental health counseling at Rockwood-based clinic. Volunteers perform medical care and administration. Portland, SE.

- LifeWorks Northwest. Provides high quality prevention, mental health and addiction services to children, teens, families, adults and older adults. Children's Relief Nursery focuses on child abuse prevention services, mental health, addiction and prevention services. Volunteers work in childcare, nurseries, schools.

- Lines for Life. Crisis lines for people with addiction, mental health and suicide intervention services, treatment referral and drug prevention education. Volunteers answer calls on Crisis Lines-Suicide Prevention and Military Helpline.

- Luke-Dorf, Inc. Serves adults with mental illness across 26 locations in greater Portland. Sponsors North Star Clubhouse mental health recovery program. Volunteers help in activities ranging from engaging individuals in healthy activities to fundraising.

- Morrison Child and Family Services. Provides mental health, substance abuse and prevention services for children from birth through age 18.

- NAMI Multnomah. Serves people with mental illness and their families through support, education, and advocacy in Multnomah County. Volunteers teach, lead groups, and participate in events and fundraising.

- Serendipity Center Children & Youth Education. Helps at-risk children and their families; certified children's mental health provider. Volunteers help in classrooms in the garden and at special events.

- William Temple House. Provides immediate emergency social services and long-term solutions through mental health counseling and 1:1 dialogue case management services. Volunteers work in thrift store and food pantry, and in dialog and case management.

- Volunteers of America Oregon. Finds innovative solutions to our community's most intractable social problems. Comprehensive programs focus on children and family, public safety/substance abuse treatment, and senior services.

Disability Services

The following is a list of non-profits and government agencies that provide services to disabled individuals. Programs may require background checks of volunteers. Visit their websites for more information.

- Bustin Barriers. Provides safe physical activities and meaningful socialization experiences for individuals with disabilities, creating opportunities for participants to have fun and strive toward their personal best. Volunteers assist with program and camp activities.

- Clark County Volunteer Connections. Connects individuals to volunteer service at places such as local Senior Centers, food pantries, youth and family oriented programs, homelessness programs, and hospitals, schools and nursing homes, and agencies that serve seniors, low-income families and kids, and provide emergency assistance.

- Clackamas County Volunteer Connection. Links volunteers with social service programs that assist seniors, people with disabilities, residents lacking resources and others in need of social services.

- Community Vision, Inc. Offers a network of services, including supported living, home ownership, asset development, youth programs and employment services for disabled individuals. Volunteers are mentors, provide house painting, yard work, work parties, work special events.

- Exceed Enterprises. Provides vocational and personal development services for people with disabilities. Volunteers work in offices, at events; provides services to disabled individuals.

- Incight. Offers programs to help people with disabilities realize their potential and encourage inclusion. Supports and empowers key life aspects of education, employment, and independence. Volunteers help deliver programs and events.

- Mt. Hood Kiwanis Camp. Partners with the U.S. Forest Service to provide individuals with disabilities an outstanding overnight recreational opportunity in the Mt. Hood National Forest. Volunteers help in work parties, at camps, in work parties and on projects and events.

- Multnomah County Aging, Disability and Veterans Services. Serves older adults (age 60 and older), people with disabilities age 18 and older, and veterans. Helps individuals identify resources to enable and promote independence, dignity and choice. Volunteers serve on Disability Advisory Council.

- Off The Couch Events. A socialization/educational program for differently-abled young adults in a non-competitive, non-threatening environment. Sponsored by Norwest Down Syndrome Association. Volunteers work on Buddy Walk event, help with social events and advocacy, learning and education and office support.

- Oregon Disability Sports. Provides and promotes recreational, fitness and competitive opportunities for people with physical disabilities. Volunteer at numerous tournaments, events and practices.

- PHAME Academy. Inspires individuals with developmental disabilities to lead full, creative lives through arts education and performance. Integrates students into artistic mainstream of visual arts, creative writing, acting, music, dance and theater.

- Quadriplegics United Against Dependency. Provides affordable, barrier-free housing and a unique model of resident-directed shared attendant care services at four buildings throughout Portland.

- Ride Connection. Provides responsive, accessible transportation options for older adults and people with disabilities, as well as community transportation solutions. Volunteers are drivers, ride ambassadors; help in office, on committees, or with advocacy and advisory councils.

- Special Olympics Oregon. Sports competition for disabled youth. Volunteers help with sports competitions; coach and train as unified partners.

- Store-to-Door. Volunteers deliver groceries from store to seniors and people with disabilities.

- Washington County Disability, Aging, and Veteran Service. Provides programs and services to maintain and enhance the quality of life to assure that basic needs are met for Washington County seniors, veterans and people with disabilities. Volunteers serve on advisory council, advise seniors on health insurance, work on REACH program, work in senior centers, provide Gatekeeper training, help clients enroll for benefits, and lead living well workshops.

Emergency Services

The following is a list of non-profits and government agencies that provide emergency food, shelter and other services to individuals. Programs may require background checks of volunteers. Visit their websites for more information.

- Andre Bessette Catholic Church. Downtown Portland community programs for homeless including morning and evening meals, foot care, art program and food pantry. Volunteers provide food, clothing, hospitality, sort donations and include teams, families, groups and members of community.

- American Red Cross Cascades Region. Provides emergency relief for victims of disaster and in major disasters and offers assistance to restore normal living. Conducts courses in basic aid, babysitting, disaster preparedness, water safety, first aid, CPR training.

- Mainspring. Operates food pantry and clothing pantry for qualifying children, families and seniors, transit assistance and bus passes. Volunteers drive, work in food pantry, clothing room and check-in desk.

- Mother and Child Education Center. Provides services and emergency supplies to parents in need. Volunteers work on auction committee, as board members, help with client care tasks, maternity clothes boutique.

- Northeast Emergency Food Program. Meets urgent food needs of north and northeast Portland neighbors; works to develop community access to adequate, affordable and healthy food.

- Oregon Food Bank. Works with statewide network of partner agencies to distribute emergency food to hungry families; involved in public policy advocacy, nutrition and garden education and improving community food systems. Volunteers repackage food, lead nutrition education classes, maintain learning gardens, help out in offices, work at events.

- Portland Animal Welfare Team (PAW Team). Helps keep people and pets together during difficult times of their lives. Provides vet care to the pets of the homeless and low-income in times of crisis. Volunteers set up clinics, help with data entry, events, communication, outreach and fundraising.

- Portland Police Bureau Sunshine Division. Provides food and clothing relief to Portland families and individuals in need.

- Salvation Army Cascade Division. Provides a variety of community programs and services such as food and nutrition, disaster services, community education, family services, youth programs, senior citizen clubs, emergency assistance, and shelters depending on location.

- The Father's Heart Street Ministry. Faith-based organization that helps anyone in need including homeless population of families living in vehicles, seniors, veterans, single mothers, single fathers and single individuals. Volunteers pick up donations, organize clothing, make sack lunches, serve lunch and meals for emergency (weather), special holiday food. Setup/clean up, drive and teach; fundraising, grants, special skills. Oregon City.

- Union Gospel Mission. Provides meals to homeless and people in need; provides food boxes, a dayroom with coffee and snacks, clothing, hygiene items, referral services and emergency cold weather shelter to the homeless. Volunteers serve meals, snacks or coffee, teach, work a thrift store, help at women's center.

- William Temple House. Provides immediate emergency social services and long-term solutions through mental health counseling and 1:1 dialogue case management services. Operates William Temple House Thrift Store. Volunteer opportunities in thrift store, social services, counseling.

Family and Social Services

The following is a list of non-profits and government agencies that serve families in need. Programs may require background checks of volunteers. Visit their websites for more information.

- Binky Patrol Comforting Covers for Kids. Volunteers make and distribute homemade blankets to children born HIV+, drug-addicted, infected with AIDS or other chronic and terminal illnesses, or abused, in foster care or experiencing trauma.

- Bradley Angle. A safe and welcoming refuge to recover from the trauma of domestic violence. Volunteers sort donations, prepare meals at shelter, maintain shelter and gardens.

- Catholic Charities of OR. Services to the most vulnerable, regardless of faith, such as disaster relief, housing development financial wellness, relationship issues, housing transitions, immigration legal services pregnancy support, refugee resettlement.

- Christmas Family Adoption Foundation. Provides assistance to those who would otherwise not have a holiday celebration, proving children with toys, clothing, and other necessities, and the entire family with household essentials and gift certificates for a holiday meal.

- Clackamas Service Center. Community Resources, medical, dental, clothing, homeless, meals, other services to those in need.

- Domestic Violence Resource Center. Educates, supports, and empowers survivors and their children who are affected by intimate partner violence by offering counseling, advocacy, shelter services and community outreach. Washington County.

- Jewish Family & Child Service. Provides social services that improve the lives of adults, low-income adults, adults with disabilities, seniors, families and children in the Jewish and general communities. Volunteers provide transportation, grocery shopping, food boxes and similar services.

- Jewish Federation of Greater Portland. Engaged in a leadership role within an intricate and responsive network of Jewish communal organizations. Addresses social service issues and community needs.

- Metropolitan Family Service. Supports community school programs, mentors children, delivers holiday gifts to disabled and older adults, provides transportation. Americorps National Service Network, AARP Experience Corps.

- Mother and Child Education Center. Providing services and emergency supplies to parents in need. Volunteers work on auction committee, as board members; help with client care tasks, maternity clothes boutique.

- Native American Youth and Family Center (NAYA). Services and community-based solutions, including lifelong educational opportunities, cultural identity, leadership development, elders support, homes for families, early childhood programs, and paths to financial security based on traditional tribal values.

- Northwest Children's Outreach. A faith-based organization dedicated to filling needs of area families, providing clothing, infant care products, diapers, formula and other necessities. Volunteers sort and pack orders, organize donation drives, help caseworkers, stock items.

- Northwest Family Services. Provider of services to reduce poverty such as youth programs, professional counseling, couple's classes, parenting, money management, job and placement, healthy relationship education.

- Salvation Army Cascade Division. Provides a variety of community programs and services such as food and nutrition, disaster services, community education, family services, youth programs, senior citizen clubs, emergency assistance, and shelters depending on location.

- Tualatin Valley Gleaners. Provides food, aid and other assistance to the low-income, disabled, children and elderly. Beaverton.

- Volunteers of America Oregon. Childcare, family recovery support, recovery programs, child abuse and domestic violence, senior resources and programs. Volunteer, one-time projects. Volunteer, ongoing positions.

- With Love. A Boutique for children in foster care. Supports their journey by lending safe, clean and quality clothing and supplies to children under age 5. Volunteers inspect, wash, sort and bundle clothes.

Food Banks and Gardens

The following is a list of food pantries and organizations that supply fresh food to those in need. Programs may require background checks of volunteers. Visit their websites for more information.

- Clark County Food Bank Garden. Farming program increases the amount of fresh, nutritious food distributed through 29 partner agencies across Clark County. Volunteers pull weeds, plant seeds, harvest fresh produce, lead groups of volunteers, work in food bank. Vancouver.

- Clark County Food Bank. Regional food bank that distributes 6 million pounds of food and 5 million meals a year. Partners with 34 local agencies and programs. Volunteers drive a refrigerated truck, sort perishable food and harvest vegetables on the farm. Vancouver.

- Growing Gardens. Volunteers build organic vegetable gardens at homes, schools and correctional facilities. Gives low-income residents resources and education they need to grow their own food. Volunteers build garden beds, lead teams, work with home gardener, present workshops, conduct nutrition education, mentor youth clubs and serve as classroom assistants. Portland NE.

- Multnomah County CROPS. Community farm donates harvests to the Oregon Food Bank. Troutdale.

- Oregon Food Bank. Works with statewide network of partner agencies to distribute emergency food to hungry families; involved in public policy advocacy, nutrition and garden education and improving community food systems. Volunteers repackage food, lead nutrition education classes, maintain learning gardens, help out in offices, work at events.

- Portland Food Project. Collects food donations from long-term, regular food donors from neighborhood volunteers and distributes to 19 food pantries.

- Portland Fruit Tree Project. Registers fruit-growers throughout the area to make it available to the needy. Volunteers participate in harvests, community outreach and fruit monitors.

- St. Johns Food Share. Provides food to low-income residents of Portland and surrounding area. Members pay a monthly amount, volunteer and visit twice a week to select food.

- Sunshine Pantry Sunshine Pantry. Provides food, amenities, housewares and clothing to people in need, in Beaverton, Tigard, Hillsboro, and Forest Grove. Volunteers load, unload, stock.

- Tualatin Valley Gleaners. Provides food, aid and other assistance to the low-income, disabled, children and elderly. Beaverton.

- Urban Farm Collective. Improving food security through growing, bartering and sharing food. Volunteers are gardeners, chicken keepers, compost gurus, mechanics, carpenters, graphic designers.

Hunger and Homeless Services

The following is a list of organizations that provide services to the homeless. Programs may require background checks of volunteers. Visit their websites for more information.

- Andre Bessette Catholic Church. Downtown Portland community programs for homeless including morning and evening meals, foot care, art program and food pantry. Volunteers provide food, clothing, hospitality, sort donations and include teams, families, groups and members of community.

- Blanchet House. Offers breakfast, lunch and dinner six days a week, with Sundays being a day of rest. Transitional shelter for men struggling with addictions. Volunteers work in cafe. Portland NW.

- Bridgetown Incorporated. Serves needs of homeless in downtown Portland. Night Strike program volunteers spend time with homeless under Burnside Bridge to distribute donated items. Programs for homeless kids to play and eat.

- Central City Concern. Services for homeless including housing, healthcare and recovery, employment and peer support.

- City Team Ministries. Provides hot meals, safe shelter, showers, clean clothing, recovery programs and other essential care to this city's homeless population.

- Clackamas Service Center, Community Resources, medical, dental, clothing, homeless, meals, other services to those in need.

- Council for the Homeless. Offers programs to end homelessness. Vancouver.

- Family Promise of Washington County. Provides resources and services for homeless individuals and families in Washington County. Brings faith community together to house homeless families overnight in church buildings. Families reside during the day at the Day House (Resource Center) where we help families achieve self-sufficiency. Volunteers help staff the shelter, provide a supportive environment of care, help with donations, perform office tasks, help with laundry and interact with parents and children.

- Good Neighbor Center. Homeless Shelter. Family homeless shelter. Volunteers bring dinner, are overnight hosts and meal hosts, perform yard work. Tigard.

- HomePlate Youth Services. Supports development of young people experiencing homelessness or housing instability through community building, education, access to services and resources, and youth empowerment. Hillsboro.

- Human Solutions. Provides low-income and homeless families with affordable housing, family support services, job readiness training and economic development opportunities. Volunteer opportunities include on-going commitments, seasonal and one-time projects.

- Janus Youth Programs. Serves homeless and runaway youth with immediate shelter, safe place to stay, in Portland and Vancouver. Volunteers do house and yard projects, prepare meals, help with outreach.

- JOIN. Homeless services; uses a "housing first" approach to achieve rapid re-housing. Services include outreach and engagement, housing retention, immersion programs, and basic services such as showers, storage lockers, laundry vouchers, mail pick-up, telephone access, and a place to escape the weather. Portland.

- Kids First Project. Provides the resources necessary for children experiencing homelessness to reach their full potential, freeing up time for parents to get training on job skills.

- Lift Urban Portland. Supports those in need in Northwest Portland, the Pearl District, Old Town and the West End to reduce hunger and improve the lives of low-income residents. Volunteers unload, sort and prepare food, pack backpacks, deliver food boxes, pick up food, work in vegetable gardens, teach wellness classes.

- Mainspring. Operates a food pantry and clothing pantry for qualifying children, families and seniors, transit assistance and bus passes. Volunteers drive. work in food pantry, clothing room and check-in desk.
- Neighborhood House. Programs for low-income children, families and seniors providing assistance with rent, food, employment, housing. Volunteers are senior visitors, distribute food boxes, work in community garden, yard cleanup, after-school programs. Portland.
- Northeast Emergency Food Program. Meets urgent food needs of north and northeast Portland neighbors; works to develop community access to adequate, affordable and healthy food.
- Operation Nightwatch. Operates safe hospitality centers where those on the streets can find food, socks, clothing, blankets, and medical care, as well as caring staff and volunteers who will listen to their stories and welcome them as friends.
- Outside In. Helps homeless youth and others move toward self-sufficiency. Offers food programs, dog activities, administrative, drug users health services. Connects them with resources and provides information and referrals.
- p:ear. Builds positive relationships with homeless and transitional youth ages 15 - 24 through education, art and recreation to affirm personal worth and create more meaningful and healthier lives.
- Partners for a Hunger Free Oregon. Raises awareness about hunger, connects people to nutrition programs and advocates for systemic changes that end hunger before it begins.
- Pixie Project. Adoption and rescue center, offers pet adoption, pet owner education and support and low cost and free spay and neuter and veterinary services for homeless and low-income pet owners.
- Portland Animal Welfare Team (PAW). Provides vet care to the pets of the homeless and low-income in times of crisis.
- Portland Food Project. Collects food donations from long-term, regular food donors from neighborhood volunteers and distributes to 19 food pantries.
- Portland Fruit Tree Project. Registers fruit-growers throughout the area to make it available to the needy. Volunteers participate in harvests, community outreach and fruit monitors.
- Portland Homeless Family Solutions. Helps homeless families with children move into long-term housing. Relies on volunteers every day at Goose Hollow Family Shelter (night shelter) and Thirteen Salmon Family Center (day shelter).
- Portland OIC / Opportunities Industrialization Center. Reconnects alienated at-risk youth affected by poverty, family instability and

homelessness; with high school education and with career training. Mentor and supports graduates in post-secondary education.

- Portland Police Bureau Sunshine Division. Provides food and clothing relief to Portland families and individuals in need.

- Portland Rescue Mission. Provides homeless and addiction services for women and children. Volunteers serve breakfast/lunch, welcome guests, and help clean and reset dining room; meet basic needs, answer phones, greet guests and respond to inquiries. Teach, mentor, work with children, work in operations, maintenance, office.

- Potluck in the Park. Serves a free hot meal to anyone in need, Sundays rain or shine, 52 weeks a year, at O'Bryant Square in downtown Portland.

- SnowCap Community Charities. Provides food, clothing, advocacy and other services to the poor. Portland SE.

- Street Roots. Publication published weekly; Portland's flagship publication addressing homelessness and poverty since 1998. Portland NW

- The Father's Heart Street Ministry. Faith-based organization that helps anyone in need including homeless population of families living in vehicles, seniors, veterans, single mothers, single fathers and single individuals. Volunteers pick up donations, organize clothing, make sack lunches, serve lunch and meals for emergency (weather), special holiday food. Setup/clean up, drive and teach; fundraising, grants, special skills. Oregon City.

- Transition Projects Inc. Serves people's needs while transitioning from homelessness to housing providing short-term residential programs, permanent housing, veterans services, mentor programs.

- Union Gospel Mission. Provides meals to homeless and people in need; provides food boxes, a dayroom with coffee and snacks, clothing, hygiene items, referral services and emergency cold weather shelter to the homeless. Volunteers serve meals, snacks or coffee, teach, work a thrift store, help at women's center.

- Write around Portland. Creative writing workshops in hospitals, prisons, schools, treatment centers, low income residences, homeless shelters and social service agencies. Publishes anthologies and holds readings to connect readers and writers.

Youth Programs

The following is a list of organizations that provide services to the youth, including underserved youth, in our communities. Many organizations require criminal and background checks of volunteers. Visit their websites for more information.

- AC (Active Children) Active Children Portland keeps children active through sports, creative writing, nutrition education, and service learning projects. Volunteers sell raffle tickets at sports events; are assistant coaches and writing/service learning mentors, and work at special events.

- Aperture Project. Engages young people through the medium of photography and creative writing, helping them express themselves in new ways, exploring their everyday lives and that of other young people.

- Big Brothers Big Sisters Columbia Northwest. Provides children experiencing adversity with strong and enduring, professionally supported one-to-one relationships. Portland.

- Caldera Caldera. A catalyst for transformation of underserved youth through innovative, year-round art and environmental programs. Volunteers provide administrative and special events support and direct services to youth.

- Camp Fire Columbia. Partners with local kids, schools and families to provide programs that support academic achievement, build social and life skills, foster community engagement, and develop career and college readiness. Volunteers help with fundraising, clean up parties at Camp Nanamu, work at food pantries, help youth with career paths.

- CASA (Court Appointed Special Advocates) for Children. When a child who has been abused and neglected is going through the trauma of the court system, a CASA advocate tirelessly works to guide them through safely, quickly, and effectively. Volunteers are trained CASA advocates.

- Chelsea Hicks Foundation. Chelsea's Closet is a rolling dress-up closet that provides monthly dress-up parties for seriously ill children at Randall Children's Hospital and Doernbecher Children's Hospital.

- Children's Book Bank. Gathers thousands of new and gently-used books from the community; cleans, repairs and sorts donated books; creates individual book bags for children without books of their own at home.

- Children's Center. A private, non-profit child abuse intervention center; children are referred to the Center for concern of sexual abuse, physical abuse, neglect and emotional abuse. Volunteers serve on committees and Board of Directors, as advocates, and support events.

- Children's Healing Art Project. CHAP teaching artists lead art adventures for children and their families at Doernbecher Children's Hospital, Knight

Cancer Institute, the OHSU Pediatric Neurosurgery Clinic and Schnitzer Diabetes Health Center.

- Children's Relief Nursery, a program of LifeWorks. Provides cost-effective child abuse prevention services. Provides mental health, addiction and prevention services.

- Community Music Center. Provides opportunities for all ages to learn about, make and enjoy music through affordable music classes and low-cost concerts, workshops and instrument rentals. Program of Portland Parks & Recreation.

- Financial Beginnings. Partners with schools, community organizations and other nonprofits to deliver age appropriate financial education. Volunteers present financial programs in schools grades 4-12.

- Focus on Youth. Provides mentoring and hands on learning experiences for disadvantaged and homeless youth. Offers Seeds of Hope, a youth leadership program incorporating science, math, photography and sustainable gardening. Volunteers help students build and plant gardens, teach photography and take youth on photography field trips.

- Foster Closet, Inc. Provides aid to the foster care community by supplying clothing and other items free of charge to children in foster care.

- Friends of the Children. Provides the most vulnerable children a nurturing and sustained relationship with a professional mentor who teaches positive values. Volunteers provide tutoring and event support.

- Girls Inc. of the Pacific Northwest. Inspires girls, ages 6-18, to be strong, smart and bold. Gender-specific programs provide girls with confidence and self-esteem for a bright and economically-independent future. Volunteers are media and STEM professionals, mentors, guest speakers and trip hosts.

- Growing Gardens. Volunteers build organic vegetable gardens at homes, schools and correctional facilities. Supports low-income residents with resources and education needed to grow their own food. Volunteers build garden beds, lead teams, work with home gardener, present workshops, nutrition education, youth clubs, classroom assistants. Portland NE.

- Harper's Playground. Creates innovative playgrounds for people of all abilities. Playground conversions.

- HOBY Oregon - Hugh O'Brian Youth Leadership. Provide youth selected by their schools to participate in unique leadership training, service-learning and motivation-building experiences.

- I Have A Dream Foundation Oregon. Addresses problem of low graduation rates among disadvantaged and low-income youth, adopting a low-income school serving highest poverty neighborhood. Volunteers mentor youth and host field trips at places of business.

- Janus Youth Programs, Inc. Sponsors programs for youth who have runaway or are homeless, been trafficked for sex, teen parents and youth living in low-income neighborhoods. Volunteers work on yard and house projects, prepare meals at youth shelters, and work in outreach.

- Kids First Project. Brings programs and services to homeless youth at local organizations. Includes storytelling, crafts, active games and other programs. Volunteers interact with children; help with background work.

- Metropolitan Family Service. Supports community school programs, mentors children, delivers holiday gifts to disabled and older adults, provides transportation, works at fundraising. Americorps National Service Network, AARP Experience Corps.

- Metropolitan Youth Symphony. Provides music for underserved schools learning an instrument for first time. Performances for low-income and under-served schools.

- Minds Matter of Portland. Transforms lives of accomplished high school students from low-income families by broadening their dreams and preparing them for college success. Volunteers mentor students.

- OHDC YouthSource. Assist youth to obtain their educational credentials while receiving support services, high school credit courses, employment training and job development services. Serves SE Washington County.

- Open Meadow Alternative Schools, Inc. An alternative college-prep program for kids who have fallen the furthest behind. Volunteers are tutors, guest speakers and work behind the scenes.

- Outside In. Helps homeless youth and others move toward improved health and self-sufficiency. Services include housing, education, employment, counseling, medical care, healthy means, recreation and safety.

- p:ear. Builds positive relationships with homeless and transitional youth ages 15 - 24 through education, art and recreation to affirm personal worth and create more meaningful and healthier lives.

- Playworks Pacific Northwest. Improves the health and well-being of children by increasing opportunities for physical activity and safe, meaningful play.

- Portland Community Football Club. Youth soccer club in Portland which has open acceptance policy for Lesbian, Gay, Bisexual, Transgender and Queer (LGBTQ) players, coaches, staff and families.

- Portland OIC / Opportunities Industrialization Center. Reconnects alienated at-risk youth affected by poverty, family instability and homelessness; with high school education and with career training. Mentor and supports our graduates in post-secondary education.

- Rock 'n' Roll Camp for Girls. Builds girls' self-esteem through music creation and performance. Provides workshops and technical training, creates leadership opportunities; cultivates supportive community of peers and mentors; encourages social change, development of life skills.

- Sauvie Island Center. Educates kids about food, farming and the land. Volunteers lead small groups of preschool through high school-aged students through interactive, hands-on, farm-based lessons.

- Schoolhouse Supplies. Volunteer-run Free Store for Teachers, stocked with supplies donated by the community, the Tools for Schools backpack giveaway, and Schoolhouse Supplies Online programs.

- SMART Program (Metro Area). Adult volunteers help children learn to read. Volunteers are paired with children for two, one-on-one 30-minute reading sessions.

- STAGES Performing Arts Youth Academy. Offers performing arts programs for children and young adults including performing arts classes and workshops. Volunteers design and construct costumes and serve on the board and various committees.

- The Dougy Center. Provides support in a safe place where children, teens, young adults and families grieving a death can share their experiences. Volunteers facilitate groups, help in office, do yard, building maintenance, help with programs, fundraising, marketing, speaking and training.

- The Portland Kitchen. A no-fee, comprehensive year-long after-school culinary program to low-income and at-risk youth ages 14-18. Provides no-cost four-day-per-week summer program.

- Vibe of Portland. Offers affordable visual arts and music classes to low-income neighborhoods through in-school, afterschool and studio classes and camps. Volunteers teach classes, help at workshops, put on shows.

- Volunteers of America Oregon. Comprehensive programs focus on children and family, public safety/substance abuse treatment and senior services.

- Washington County Kids Fund. Invests in child abuse prevention, high-quality early childhood care, education and hunger fighting.

- Youth Progress Association. Provides youth with the living skills, structure and support needed to transition successfully into the community. Serves highest risk youth.

APPENDIX F: CYCLING RESOURCES

• Cycling Places and Resources by County • Cycling Clubs, Meetups, Events

The following are lists of area cycling places and resources by county, clubs and Meetups, and annual cycling events. Visit their websites for more information.

Cycling Places and Resources by County

The following list contains a lineup of cycling resources in Clackamas, Clark, Multnomah and Washington Counties.

Clackamas County

• Look no further than the *Bike It! Map. Bike It!* is a full-color, full-size, water resistant map with the entire County on one side and the urban areas on the other. The map helps bicyclists pick the best work or recreation routes, and includes 0 suggested recreation rides. It includes hard-surfaced and gravel roads in the Mt. Hood National Forest, and lists single- and double-track mountain bike trails. Purchase for $5.00.

Clackamas County, City of Milwaukee

• *Bike map.*

Clark County

• The City of Vancouver *Bike Map*, shows the city's multi-use paths, shared roadways, bike lanes, and difficult connections, steep grades, and other areas to be aware of, as well as cyclists prohibited streets. Vancouver Parks and Rec provides map of Clark County trails, information on regional parks, and how to cross the I-5 Bridge and travel through Jantzen Beach and Delta Park.

Multnomah County, Portland

• *Interactive bike maps* provided by the City of Portland help cyclists find the best routes to get around Portland – low traffic streets, intersections with traffic signals, bike shops, and more. Click the link, and the neighborhood location. Multi-languages. Citywide map includes resources for bike travelers, such as group ride contacts, safety programs, bike rentals, bike parking, bicycling tips and more.

• City of Portland. *Senior Recreation Catalog.* Offers seasonal outdoor activities including group rides and workshops. All levels of participation.

Multnomah County, Gresham

- *Bicycle maps* show bicycle routes and their connections to other cities such as Portland, Fairview, Wood Village and Troutdale. Bike wayfinding signs are along major city bike routes. Get maps and guide on line, or on water-resistant paper at Gresham City Hall.

Washington County

- City of Beaverton. *Bike Map.*
- City of Tigard. Download free bike maps or stop by city offices.
- Hillsboro Bike Maps. Rock Creek Trail.
- Forest Grove. *Forest Grove Bike Maps.*
- Tualatin Hills. Trails maps.
- Tualatin-Sherwood. *Bike Map.*

Other Resources

- *Bike Portland.* An independent daily news source that covers the Portland bike scene.

- *Metro Bike There.* On-line map of bikeways, safer streets, bike lanes and more of the entire Portland metro area.

- *PDOT, Bicycle Portland.* A website of maps, classes, guides and lots more for safe cycling around PDX.

- *Ride Oregon.* A website of cycling destinations, clubs, events and resources.

Cycling Clubs, Meetups, Events

The following is a list of list area cycling clubs.

- Beaverton Bicycle Club. Competitive racing.
- Northwest Trail Alliance. Mountain biking advocacy, trail stewardship and riding group.
- Oregon Human Powered Vehicles. Group of fun-loving recumbent bike and trike riders.
- Oregon Randonneurs. Club of long-distance cyclists.
- Portland Velo Cycling Club. Caters largely to racers, or spearing racers, who are masers-category eligible and looking to be part of a supportive, innovative and experienced team. Weekly rides and event rides for members.

- Portland Wheelmen Touring Club. 600-member recreational riding and social organization for bicyclists all abilities. Year-round events.
- Shift. A loose-knit, informal bunch of bike-loving folks. Plans, executes, publicizes, and get involved in celebration of bicycle events. Calendar.
- Sorella Forte Cycling Club. Open to all women who share a passion for riding a bike — ANY bike; race and recreational riders.
- Trails Club of Oregon. Trails Club Bicycling. Schedules recreational rides and bike tours in and out of Greater Portland.

- Vancouver Bicycle Club. Recreational bicycling and social organization.

Cycling also is an activity of other outdoor groups, such as those who hike, ski, kayak, etc.):

- Cascade Prime Timers
- Endorphin Drip Hiking and Cycling Club
- Multiple Outdoor Activities for Boomers
- Trails Club of Oregon

Cycling Meetup Groups

The following lists cycling Meetup groups that may appeal to Boomers.

- CycleManiacs. Social rides, all skill levels.
- Go the Distance. Cycling with friends. Regular rides around Portland.
- Ladies Let's Ride. Members just like to ride bikes, chat, improve fitness and become safer riders.
- Northwest Butts on Bikes. Recreational easy-going rides.
- Out Spoke'n. Recreational cycling club for Lesbian, Gay, Bisexual, and Transgender community and their friends.
- Performance Great Ride Series: Tualatin. Rides of 12 to 15 miles around Tualatin from Performance Bicycle.
- Performance Great Ride Series: Portland. Rides of 12 to 15 miles around Portland from Performance Bicycle.
- Portland Area Recreational Cyclists. Cycles on paved and mountain bike trails. All levels.
- Ride Like a Girl. Women of all bicycling abilities.
- SE Portland Mural Art Bicycling Meetup. Tours that will guide cyclists to colorful, playful, and sometimes thought-provoking examples of local mural art.

- Team Orenco Cycling. All levels, family friendly.
- Whinos (easy-going rides in wine county).

Annual Cycling Events

The following is a list of popular cycling events in the Portland area, including the event month.

- Worst Day of the Year Ride. Regardless of the weather, thousands of fun-loving cyclists grab their friends, don costumes, ride their bikes and wave silly flags. February.

- Sunday Parkways. Held in several different neighborhoods each year, Sunday Parkways rides convert city streets into car-free zones, encouraging cyclists to explore different parts of the city. Each event features stops in city parks along the route, with entertainment, food and activities. May-September.

- Filmed by Bike Festival. Short films about bicycling. Portland NE. May.

- Reach the Beach. Scenic ride from Portland to Pacific Ocean 28, 55, 80, or 100 miles. May.

- Bridge Pedal. Pedal fancy- and car-free with nearly 20,000 other cyclists across Portland's Willamette River bridges – Sellwood to the St. Johns and most others in between. August.

- World Naked Bike Ride. This could have, but didn't, originate in Portland, one of 74 ride-in-the-buff cities from Amsterdam to Perth. June.

- Padalpalooza. Multiple anything goes, free-for-all rides bike festival. 3 weeks of bicycle events including scavenger hunts, costume rides, casual tours, pub crawls, and naked bicycle ride. June.

- Beaverton Banks and Beyond Tour. 64-, 86-, 100-mile options going through Banks, the Vernonia Trail, and beyond. August.

- Handmade Bike & Beer Festival. Brings together two of Portland's favorite activities for one exciting weekend family-friendly mash up. October.

APPENDIX G: FITNESS PLACES AND RESOURCES

• Outdoor Clubs • Running Clubs • Aquatics Centers • Pickleball and Tennis • Community Colleges, Parks & Rec, YMCA • Fitness Clubs and Meetups

The following are listings of area fitness resources including outdoor activities, places to swim, run and jog, play tennis and pickleball, and other fitness places such as community and senior centers, community colleges and parks and recreation facilities. Visit their websites for more information.

Outdoor Clubs

The following is a list of outdoor clubs and groups that sponsor Boomer-friendly hike, walk, snowshoe, x-country ski and similar activities.

- Bergfreunde Ski Club. Outdoor activities including snowshoeing, cross-country skiing and hiking.
- Cascade Prime Timers. Age 50+ actives who hike, ski, snowshoe, kayak, cycle, and travel.
- Clark County Running Club. Invites walkers to share their running routes.
- Friends of the Columbia River Gorge. Nature advocates who sponsor hikes.
- Mazamas. A mountaineering education club that also sponsors walks, hikes, ski, snowshoe.
- Oregon Nordic Club Portland. Promotes cross-country skiing.
- Oregon Road Runners Club. Invites walkers to share their running routes.
- Oregon Sierra Club. Environmental advocates; also sponsors hikes.
- Oregon Wild. Advocate for Oregon wildlands; also sponsors hikes, ski, snowshoe.
- Oregon Walks. Sponsors neighborhood walks; promotes walking and making conditions for walking safe, convenient and attractive.
- Portland Fit. Invites walkers to share their running routes.
- Portland Walking Tours. Offers specialty themed walking tours of unique places around Portland.
- Positively Portland. Walking tours that explore architecture, history and culture of Portland area.

- Racewalkers Northwest. Practices the race walking technique for fitness and competition.
- Ten Toe Express. Free guided walks held from May through September, sponsored by Portland Bureau of Transportation.
- Trails Club of Oregon. Year-round activities, hiking, biking, snow sports.
- Uniquely Portland. Walking tours and day trips in and around Portland.

Running Clubs

The following is a list of age-friendly running clubs that welcome all abilities to group runs and walk/run events.

- Clark County Running Club. Regular running events for members. All ages and abilities, new or experienced. Walkers welcome.
- Fleet Feet. Community classes and fun runs.
- Foot Traffic. Regular outings for running and walkers with various distance routes.
- Gresham Running Club. All abilities, distances, and goals welcomed. Free, supported with shirt purchases. Weekly track and road runs.
- Molalla Running Club. Promotes healthy lifestyles through group runs; sponsors local road races.
- NoPo Runnings. Good workouts, good brews, all ability levels.
- Oregon Road Runners Club. Promotes running and walking for health; sponsors group training runs and events.
- Portland Fit. Marathon and half marathon training for a fee.
- Portland Frontrunners. Running club for lesbians, gays, bisexuals, transgender and queer individuals and their friends in Portland area. Recreational to serious training.
- Portland Running Company. Hosts a variety of free weekly group runs for all abilities and interests.
- Team Red Lizard. Offers a training, racing, and social network for athletes of all abilities. Weekly group runs.

Aquatics Centers

The following are lists of community pools and aquatics centers by county that offer adult lap swim and instruction.

Clackamas County

- North Clackamas Parks & Recreation District. Aquatics Center fitness classes in seasonal catalog. Lap swim.
- Clackamas Community College. Water exercise and fitness classes listed in Community Education catalog, 3 locations.

- City of Oregon City. Water exercise programs; see Swimming Pool page.
- Sherwood Regional Family YMCA. Lap pool, water exercise. Website, Aquatics page.

Clark County

- Clark County Family YMCA. Adult swim lessons. Aquatics page of website.
- Vancouver Parks & Recreation. 3 pools, water exercise classes.
- Vancouver Public Schools. Propstra Aquatic Center. All ages. Adult swim lessons.

Multnomah County

- City of Gresham, Aquatic Centers, Mt. Hood Community College, Gresham High School. Water fitness, adult programs and lessons.
- City of Portland, Oregon. Swim Pool and Lessons page. Deep, shallow, and moving water fitness classes. See Recreation catalog; links to local pools, check local pool schedule.

Washington County

- City of Forest Grove Aquatics Center. Adult lessons and fitness classes.
- City of Hillsboro Shute Park Aquatic Center. Adult lessons, fitness classes.
- City of Sherwood. 4 outdoor pools.
- City of Tigard pool. Check Activity Guide for swim schedule.
- Tigard-Tualatin Aquatic District. Adult lessons, fitness exercise.
- Portland Community College. Sylvania Campus. Adult swim classes. Community Education catalog.
- Tualatin Hills Parks and Recreation. 8 community pools. Adult lessons and aquatic fitness, open swim.
- Sherwood Regional Family YMCA. 25 yard, 3 lane pool. Water fitness.

Pickleball and Tennis

The following is a list of places where you can learn and play tennis and pickleball in your city or county.

Pickleball

- See schedules and facilities at The *Pickleball Press* Facebook page and the Portland Area Pickleball Schedule.

Tennis

Clackamas County

- North Clackamas Parks & Recreation District. Find a Park search. Tennis courts at Century Park, Milwaukee, and Risley Park, Oak Grove.

- City of Oregon City. Parks Amenities search. Tennis courts at D. C. Latourette Park, Hartke Park, Hillendale Park, and Rivercrest Park.

Clark County

- Vancouver Tennis Center. Adult group lessons.
- Vancouver Parks & Recreation. Find a Park search. Courts at Fisher Basin Park, Oakbrook Park.

Multnomah County

- City of Portland, Oregon. Parks & Recreation, Tennis page on website. Portland Tennis Center, 8 indoor, 4 outdoor courts. Senior tennis pass. Senior Mixers held every week day. Lessons. St. Johns Racquet Center. Adult lessons.
- Portland Community College. Community Education catalog.

Washington County

- Beaverton. Babette Horsenstein Tennis Center. 6 indoor, 8 outdoor, 1 stadium court. Adult lessons.
- City of Hillsboro. Parks with tennis courts: 53rd Avenue Community Park, Magnolia Park, Reedville Creek Park, Rood Bridge Park, Shute Park, and Turner Creek Park.
- City of Sherwood. Tennis courts at Henson Park, Indianhead Park.
- City of Tigard. Tennis courts at Summerlake Park.
- City of Tualatin. Tennis courts at Atfalati, Ibach and Community Parks.
- Portland Community College. Community Education catalog.

Community Colleges, Parks & Rec, YMCA

The following is a list of community college, parks and recreation programs and YMCAs that offer senior fitness programs.

- Beaverton Hoop YMCA. Active older adult fitness classes; senior circuit machines, stretching, cardio and flexibility.
- Clackamas County Community College. See Community Education catalog. Exercise and swimming classes. 65+ may qualify for senior discount.
- Clark College. Community Education. Class Schedule offers health exercise programs such as yoga, dancing, weight loss.
- Clark County Family YMCA. Active older adult fitness classes; strength, aerobics, yoga, stretching, water exercise.
- Hillsboro Parks & Recreation. Activities Guide. Offers health and fitness and exercise programs at Shute Park Aquatic & Recreation Center for all ages; Senior Center wellness programs. Senior discounts.
- North Clackamas Parks and Recreation District. See Discovery Guide for adult fitness classes, exercise, seasonal sports and recreation.

- Oregon City Parks & Recreation Department. Classes through Pioneer Senior Center.

- Portland Community College. Community Education schedule. Browse schedule for fitness workouts, classes and training, exercise sports at facilities in Multnomah and Washington Counties.

- Portland Parks & Recreation. Senior Recreation Catalog. Health, fitness, exercise programs at 5 community centers; Senior Active Passes.

- Sherwood Regional Family YMCA, Active older adult fitness classes, yoga and strength training, water exercise.

- Tualatin Hills Park & Recreation District. Activities Guide. Elsie Stuhr Center, group fitness classes, all levels. Fitness equipment and classes at three other locations. See current Activities Guide. Senior discounts.

- Vancouver Parks & Recreation. Select Catalog Activity Guide. Fitness Center and 50 + fitness classes at the Firstenburg Community Center.

Fitness Clubs and Meetups

The following is a list of fitness-related clubs and Meetups with healthy outdoor activities that may appeal to Boomers.

- Beaverton Nature Walks
- Eastside Women's Fitness
- Multiple Outdoor Activities for Boomers (MOAB)
- Oregon City/Beavercreek Women's Hiking/Outdoors
- PNW Women's Outdoor Group, Hiking in the Pacific Northwest
- Portland Veggie Hikers
- PDX Metro Pack Walks (w/dogs)
- Ride Like a Girl Cycling
- River West Village Senior Walks
- Rose City Wanderers
- Trails Club of Oregon
- Walking Oregon and SW Washington
- Walk with Friends Hillsboro
- Why Not Fitness
- Yoga in the Park – East Vancouver/Camas

Meetups come, go and change. Find current meetup descriptions and schedules at Meetup.com. Search by city, then by interest such as fitness, exercise, walking, hiking, etc. Sign up and show up.

APPENDIX H: GARDENING PLACES AND RESOURCES

• Public and Demonstration Gardens • Garden Friends Groups • Community Gardens • Garden Clubs • Events and Shows • Classes, Workshops, Seminars

The following are listings of resources for gardeners. Visit their websites for more information.

Public and Demonstration Gardens

The following contains listings of public and demonstration gardens by county which include friends of groups and volunteers. Visit their websites for more information.

Clackamas County

- Clackamas Community College Demonstration Garden. Model garden to teach about issues related to low water use landscapes – soil enhancements, the right plant/right place, selection of low water use plants, mulching, maintenance, and efficient irrigation. Oregon City.

- Home Orchard Society Arboretum. A 1.6-acre demonstration orchard maintained by the society; showcases heirloom fruit varieties, organic orchard practices, cultural techniques, and more. Fruit growing events and information. Welcomes volunteers of all skill levels. Oregon City.

- Roger Clematis Garden. Contains the most comprehensive collection of clematis within a public garden in North America. Join/Volunteer. Supported by Friends of Clematis Collection. West Linn.

- Secret Garden Growers. Garden within a country nursery. 8 acres, path to pond and creek, whispering trees. Canby.

Clark County

- Esther Short Rose Garden. Esther Short Park. 5 acres feature Victorian Rose Gardens. Volunteer for Vancouver Parks. Vancouver.

- Fort Vancouver Heritage Garden. Fort Vancouver. Features heirloom vegetables herbs and flowers. National park with a rich cultural past. Volunteer-In-Parks program.

- Wildlife Botanical Garden. Naturescaping of Southwest Washington. Gardens and gardeners demonstrate and teach gardening concepts that attract birds, butterflies, hummingbirds and other wildlife to residential gardens. Volunteers work on garden tasks, equipment repair, teaching, coordinating activities. Brush Prairie, WA.

Multnomah County

- Elk Rock Gardens at the Bishop's Close. A hillside estate overlooking Willamette River. Magnolias and other native and non-native trees, shrubs and plants. Gardens support by Friends of Elk Rock Gardens. Portland SW.

- Blue Lake Natural Discovery Garden. Blue Lake Park. Smell the flowers, touch the leaves and feel inspired by this peaceful, playful demonstration garden. Volunteer through Metro.

- Crystal Springs Rhododendron Garden. Outdoor Rhododendron garden. Volunteers from American Rhododendron Society, Friends of Crystal Springs Rhododendron Garden and Master Gardeners program. Care for the grounds, work on garden education and events. Portland SE.

- Hoyt Arboretum. 189 ridge-top acres in Washington Park accessible by trails. Includes 6,000 specimens from around the world. Friends group; corporate or work group volunteers work on garden crews, trail and tree maintenance, guide tours, perform research and more. Portland SW.

- International Rose Test Garden. Washington Park Rose Garden with over 7,000 rose plants of approximately 550 varieties. Volunteer for garden and non-garden tasks. Portland SW.

- Ladd Circle Rose Gardens. Neighborhood rose garden. Cared for by Friends of Ladd's Addition Gardens. Portland SE.

- Lan Sue Chinese Garden. Tranquil botanical garden featuring rare plants native to China. Portland NW.

- Leach Botanical Garden. Contains several discrete collections with a focus on the flora of Oregon. Volunteers welcome visitors, provide tours, care for plants and trails, stage events and fundraisers. Portland SE.

- Legacy Healing Gardens. Legacy Good Samaritan Medical Center (Stenzel Healing Garden); Legacy Emanuel Medical Center (Oregon Burn Center Garden and Emanuel Terrace Garden); Legacy Mount Hood Medical Center Healing Garden. Guided tours and open garden events. Volunteers help with garden maintenance, clerical work and assist with events.

- Peninsula Park Rose Garden. Neighborhood rose garden. Cared for by Friends of Peninsula Park Rose Garden. Portland N.

- Portland Japanese Garden. A 5.5-acre haven of tranquil beauty nestled in the scenic west hills. Volunteers assist with gallery exhibitions and cultural festivals. Portland SW.

- Portland Memory Garden. Designed for the special needs of those with memory disorders to provide respite for their caregivers. Open to public. Friends of the Portland Memory group cares for gardens. Portland SE.

- Sauvie Island Center. Educates kids about food, farming and the land. Volunteers: Lead small groups of school children through interactive lessons on pollination, healthy soil, planting, etc.

- Sauvie Island Lavender Farm. Working farm on Sauvie Island with 800 plants of 14 varieties.

- The Grotto. A place of solitude, peace and prayer. National Catholic Shrine. Botanical garden, rock cave carved into base of 110-ft cliff. Volunteers maintain pathways, shrubs, flower bed, and paved areas, help set up special events such as Festival of Lights, sell merchandise. Portland NE.

- Tryon Life Community Farm. Demonstration garden focused on food production using standard organic and permaculture techniques; primarily annuals, small perennials. Volunteer work parties. Portland SE.

Washington County

- Cooper Mountain Demonstration Garden. Colorful, low-maintenance, wildlife-friendly plants. Volunteer through Metro. Beaverton.

- Jenkins Estate. Wooded, wild natural growth areas, cultivated plants and a tamed landscape of ornamental trees, shrubs, flowers, winding pathways. Rhododendron, perennial, rock, and herb garden and rose pergola.

- Legacy Healing Gardens. Legacy Meridian Park Medical Center, Lewis & Floetta Ide Healing Garden. Volunteers help with garden maintenance, clerical work and assisting with events. Tualatin.

- Lloyd Baron Rhododendron Garden at Rood Bridge Park. Hundreds of species, hybrid rhododendrons, trees and companion plants. Celebrates the gardener, horticulturist and the art of landscape design. Volunteer for Hillsboro parks. Hillsboro.

- Portland Community College-Rock Creek Learning Garden. Provides experiential education and life-long learning opportunities for PCC students, faculty, staff and community members.

- Tualatin Hills Parks & Recreation. Gardening work parties at Historic Jenkins Estate and Tualatin Hills Nature Center. Pruning, weeding, propagating native plants.

Other

- Oregon Gardens. Lush 80-acre botanical garden with amphitheater, tours and a Frank Lloyd Wright house. South of Portland. Individual, group volunteers for garden work, special events.

Garden Friends Groups

Gardens with friends groups include:

- Bishop's Close Elk Rock Gardens
- Crystal Springs Rhododendron Garden
- Ladd's Addition Gardens
- Peninsula Park Rose Garden
- Roger Clematis Collection

Community Gardens

The following is a list of area community gardens by county. Visit their websites for more information.

Clackamas County

- Canby Community Gardens. Baker Prairie Community Garden, Canby Center Community Garden, St. Patrick's Community Garden, United Methodist Community Garden.

- Clackamas Community College Gardens. Spaces available on campus to create mini gardens, grow vegetables, fruits and flowers. Oregon City Campus.

- Luscher Farm Community Garden. Lake Oswego.

- Wilsonville Community Garden. Memorial Park. In-ground plots, raised beds, water, deer fence.

Clark County

- Clark County's Heritage Farm, Hazel Dell.

- Community Grown. Website of community gardening topics and locations in Clark County.

- Vancouver Community Gardens. Marshall Community Park Garden, Haagen Community Park Garden, Campus Garden, Ellsworth Road Garden, Fruit Valley Park.

- Urban Abundance. Helping to harvest and tend Clark County's home orchards; offers tools for community to register fruit and nut trees, volunteers help with harvest.

Multnomah County

- Friends of Portland Community Gardens. Supports and expands community gardening opportunities for all Portland-area residents to grow healthy food and build community. Supports Portland Parks & Recreation Community Gardens programs. Membership fee.

- Gresham Community Gardens. Four garden locations: City Hall, Yamhill, Thom Park, Nadaka Nature Park and Garden.

- Growing Gardens. Helps people grow their own food. Builds organic, raised bed vegetable gardens in yards and balconies.

- Grow Portland. Transforms underused spaces in city to gardens. Offers spaces in Cesar Chavez East County, Eastminster and Floyd Light Community Gardens. Classes.

- Portland Community Gardens. 50 gardens located throughout the city, developed and operated by volunteers and parks and recreation staff, offering a variety of activities.

- Urban Farm Collective. Land owners provide land for neighborhood run gardens; harvests bartered at weekly market. Transforms vacant lots into neighborhood food gardens for education and research into sustainable agriculture.
- Village Gardens. Includes individual and family garden plots. Resident-led vegetable gardens and 30 fruit/nut tree orchard in Cathedral Gardens.

Washington County

- Beaverton Community Gardens. Three sites where residents come together to grow food, community and sense of place. Beaverton Community Center building, Kennedy Gardens, Welch-Centennial Gardens.
- Cedar Creek Church. Sherwood.
- Forest Grove Gardens. Victory Garden.
- Hillsboro Church Gardens. Reedville Presbyterian, Alliance Bible.
- Hillsboro Community Gardens. Four organic, pesticide-free gardens, over 200 community gardeners, and a total of nearly two acres of organic food production. Calvary Community Garden, Sonrise Community Garden, Orenco Community Garden, Davide Hill Community Garden.
- Hilltop Community Garden. Sponsor, Tualatin United Methodist Church.
- Sherwood Presbyterian Church Community Garden.
- Tigard Community Gardens. 25 garden plots: Greenfield and Jack Park Community Gardens.
- Tualatin Community Garden. Hosted by Boones Ferry Community Church.
- Tualatin Hills Parks & Rec Community Gardens. 12 garden sites. A. M. Kennedy Park, Barsotti Park, Bethany Lake Park, Cedar Hills Park, Eichler Park, Harman St. Swim Center, Howard M. Terpenning Complex, Jackie Husen Park, John Marty Park Community Organic Garden, Powerline corridor between Charlais & Somerset Dr., Ridgewood Park, Southminister Presbyterian Church, Evelyn M. Schiffler Memorial Park. Beaverton.
- Wilsonville Community Garden. Sponsor, Wilsonville Parks and Recreation.

Garden Clubs

The following is a list of garden clubs by county. Visit their websites for information.

Clackamas County

- Clackamas District Garden Clubs
- Canby Garden Club of Oregon
- Estacada Garden Club
- Happy Valley Garden Club

- Lake Grove Garden Club
- Milwaukie Garden Club
- Oak Grove Garden Club
- Oak Lodge Garden Club
- Oswego Garden Club
- Posy Pickers Garden Club
- Sandy Garden Club
- Sunny Hills
- West Linn
- Wilsonville

Clark County

- Clark County Newcomers Club-Gardening Group, Vancouver
- Community Garden Club of Camas/Washougal
- VanRidge Garden Club, Ridgefield
- West Vancouver Garden Club

Multnomah County

- Multnomah District
- Columbian Garden Club, Corbett
- Metropolitan Garden Club of Portland
- Native Plant Society of Oregon, Portland
- Night Crawlers Garden Club, Troutdale
- Oregon Cactus & Succulent Society, Portland
- Oregon Camellia Society, Portland
- Oregon Mycological Society, Portland
- Petal Pushers Garden Club, Gresham
- Portland District

- Portland Garden Club
- Portland Rose Society
- Powell Valley Garden Club, Gresham
- Ramblin' Rows Garden Club, Portland

Washington County

- Aloha Garden Club
- Pioneer District Garden Clubs

- Cedar Mill Garden Club, Beaverton
- Chehalem Garden Club
- Hillsboro Garden Club
- North Plains Community Garden Club
- Summerfield Garden Club
- Tualatin Valley Chapter of the American Rhododendron Society

Events and Shows

The following is a list of a gardens, exhibits and gardeners' workshops where you can unearth some of the newest garden ideas. Visit their websites for more information.

- Garden Time. TV show for gardeners.
- Portland Spring Home & Garden Show. Portland NE. February.
- Home & Garden Idea Fair. Ridgefield, WA. April.
- Spring Garden Fair. Plants, classes, master gardeners, potting station. Canby. April, May.
- Camas (WA) Mother's Day Plant & Garden Fair. May.
- Portland Garden Club. Flower shows and classes. Month and location vary.
- Portland Fall Home & Garden Show. Portland NE. October.

Classes, Workshops, Seminars

The following contains listings to organizations and places that offer free and inexpensive gardening classes, events and workshops, listed by county. (See also the list of area Garden Clubs on page 134, most offer gardening classes, speakers, workshops, and events.) Visit their websites for information.

Clark County

- City of Vancouver Parks. Sponsors gardening and planting workshops.
- Clark College. Community education catalog, select Recreation, Home & Garden classes.
- Green Neighbors. Department of Environmental Services. Community events related to gardens, wildlife, birds, landscaping. Vancouver, WA.
- Shorty's Garden & Home. Workshops and classes. Vancouver.
- Washington State University Master Gardener Program. Sponsors, co-sponsors with other area agencies, events, workshops and nursery tours.

Clackamas County

- Boring Square Garden. Offers gardening classes.

- Clackamas County Community College. Community Education catalog, search for gardening classes.
- Clackamas County Master Gardeners. Free Lectures and seminars; Spring Garden Fair.
- Dennis Seven Dees. Ornamental and edible gardening classes covering a wide range of topics. Lake Oswego.

Multnomah County

- Cornell Farms. Join email list for events and classes. Portland.
- Dennis Seven Dees. Ornamental and edible gardening classes covering a wide range of topics. Portland.
- Garden Fever. Ornamental and edible gardening classes - mostly hands-on craft-related topics including terrariums, flower arranging and seasonal wreathes, etc. Portland.
- Growing Gardens. Volunteers build organic vegetable gardens at homes, schools and correctional facilities and teach new gardeners. Learn and grow workshops.
- Grow Portland. Transforms underused spaces in city to gardens. Offers spaces in Cesar Chavez East County, Eastminster and Floyd Light Community Gardens. Classes.
- Hardy Plant Society of Oregon. Offers educational programs and activities year-round. Portland
- Joy Creek Nursery. A wide range of classes taught by regional and even national experts.
- Lan Su Classical Chinese Garden. Classes and programs related to Chinese culture (Feng Shui, tea, etc.) but can relate to gardening, too. Portland.
- Leach Botanical Garden. Wide range of classes relating to sustainability issues, gardening with children and more.
- Learning Gardens Laboratory. Provides garden-based education for public school students and their families and community members. Portland State University. Portland SE
- Livingscape Nursery. Edible and native plant classes, as well as food harvest and preservation.
- Portland Nursery. Wide range of ornamental and edible gardening classes and craft demos.
- Metro. Offers free presentations by renowned experts and inspiring educators to garden clubs, neighborhood associations and other community groups.

- Metro Master Gardeners. Offers the public gardening information and education opportunities. Provides research-based education and outreach about horticulture and household pests.

- Mt. Hood Community College. Community education course catalogs, search for gardening classes. Gresham.

- Multnomah County Master Gardeners. Provides science-based horticulture education offered as a hybrid course including in-person classes, online content, hands-on workshops, gardening seminars and a final exam. Portland.

- Oregon State University Master Gardener Metro Area. Provides science-based horticulture education including in-classes, online content, hands-on workshops, gardening seminars and a final exam.

- Portland Community College. Community education, search for gardening classes in current class schedule.

- Portland Fruit Tree. Neighbors share fruit harvests to combat hunger. Classes and courses on fruit tree pruning.

- Portland Japanese Garden. Periodic programs on elements of traditional Japanese gardening.

- Portland Parks & Recreation. Home & Garden Classes. Select Home & Garden from Activities list on Home page.

- West Multnomah Soil and Water Conservation District. Information on gardening with native plants. Backyard Habitat Certification Program and programs for community gardens.

- Zenger Farm. Education programs, field trips, school programs, community workshops and demonstrations and farmer training.

Washington County

- Al's Garden Center. Ornamental and edible gardening classes on a range of topics. Beaverton.

- Dennis Seven Dees. Ornamental and edible gardening classes, a wide range of topics. Beaverton.

- Farmington Gardens. Various classes and events on trees, seeds, planting, garden planting. Beaverton.

- OSU Master Gardeners Program. Educates the public about all aspects of growing and caring for plants. Washington County Master Gardeners hold a variety of demonstrations, lectures, seminars and workshops in various locations, including THPRD's Jenkins Estate and the Washington County Fairplex Demonstration Garden. Most events free and open to the public.

- Smith Berry Barn. Various gardening seminars and workshops. Hillsboro.

- The Garden Corner. Various workshops and events. Tualatin.

APPENDIX I: HEALTH AND HEALING VOLUNTEER PLACES

• Community Healthcare Organizations • Community Mental Health Programs • Health-Based Support Organizations • Hospice and End of Life Care • Hospitals and Medical Centers

The following are listings of community healthcare-related organizations that rely on volunteers, grouped by general categories. Visit their websites for more information about volunteering.

Community Healthcare Organizations

The following is a list community healthcare organizations that welcome volunteers. Programs may require background checks of volunteers. Visit their websites for more information.

- African American Health Coalition. Alliance of individuals, agencies and organizations that addresses health issues faced by African Americans. Volunteers participate in health fair, health walk, daily operations, programs and events, interviews, newsletters, blogs, office work.

- Clackamas Health Clinics. County healthcare organization providing primary care, prenatal, dental, mental health.

- Clackamas Volunteers in Medicine - The Founders Clinic. Free clinic services provided by medical and non-medical volunteers. Medical volunteers are credentialed medical personnel and allied health professionals. Non-medical volunteers provide patient advocacy, administrative support, patient contact, translation, technology, communication, building maintenance and upkeep, fundraising and events; boards and committees. Oregon City.

- Coalition of Community Health Clinics. a non-profit network of 14 safety-net health centers in the Portland area.

- Dental Foundation of Oregon. Direct care and oral health education to underserved children on the Tooth Taxi free mobile dental clinic. Volunteers are dentists, hygienists and dental assistants who enjoy working with children.

- Good News Community Health Center. Faith- and community-based health center offers primary care, diabetes education, foot care and mental health counseling at Rockwood-based clinic. Volunteers perform medical care and administration. Portland SE.

- Mercy and Wisdom Community Health Clinic. Serves uninsured and low income populations with primary care, acupuncture and Chinese medicine. Volunteers are directors, managers, professionals in healthcare, technology, and fundraising, landscapers and office workers. Portland SE.

- North by Northeast Community Health Center. Free health screening and basic medical services to medically under-served with priority to African Americans and low-income. Volunteers are clinicians, nurses, medical assistants, office workers, and gardeners; help with special projects.

- Project Access NOW. Connects low-income uninsured to donated primary and specialty care providers, hospitals, clinics and other organizations, pays premiums; transportation care seats, temporary housing. Volunteers help at events, assist in the office, serve on committees.

- Ronald McDonald House. Provides a "home away from home" for families with seriously ill children, and supports initiatives to improve pediatric health. Volunteers work with families inside the house, at special events, in leadership roles or in the community.

- Southwest Community Health Center. A safety-net-clinic providing basic health care to low-income uninsured. Volunteers provide clinical care and non-clinical support, Spanish interpretation. Hillsboro, Portland SW.

- Virginia Garcia Memorial Health Center. Provides primary health care to migrant and seasonal farm workers and others with barriers to receiving healthcare in Washington and Yamhill Counties. Volunteers assist medical teams in mobile clinic and outreach.

- Wallace Medical Concern. Provides neighborhood-based health care services and assistance for at multiple locations in East Multnomah County and the metro area. Volunteers include licensed medical providers, and those in non-medical tasks.

Community Mental Health Programs

The following is a list of area mental health programs. Programs may require background checks of volunteers. Visit their websites for more information.

- ASHA International. Promotes personal, organizational, and community wellness through mental health education, training and support. Volunteers are involved in marketing and PR, development, fundraising, grant writing, photography, social media, health and wellness.

- Baby Blues Connection. Supports women and families coping with pregnancy and postpartum mood disorders, and professionals who serve them. Volunteers provide mom-to-mom, dad, phone, mentor and email support, as well as office social media.

- Circles of Support & Accountability. Programs to heal individuals and a community after violent crime.

- Comprehensive Options for Drug Abusers. Treats people with alcohol, drug and mental health challenges. Volunteers paint CODA residences, plant gardens, make afghans, host barbecues, even organize closets, hold fundraising events.

- De Paul Treatment Centers. Provides chemical dependency treatment services to men, women, youth and families. Volunteers involved in peer support.

- Good News Community Health Center. Faith- and community-based health center offers primary care, diabetes education, mental health counseling, foot care. Volunteers perform medical care and administration.

- LifeWorks Northwest. Provides high quality prevention, mental health and addiction services to children, teens, families, adults and older adults. Children's Relief Nursery focuses on child abuse prevention services, mental health, addiction and prevention services. Volunteers work in childcare, nurseries, schools.

- Lines for Life. Crisis lines for people with addiction, mental health and suicide intervention; services, treatment referral, drug prevention education. Volunteers answer calls on helplines.

- Luke-Dorf, Inc. Serves adults with mental illness across 26 locations in greater Portland. Sponsors North Star Clubhouse mental health recovery program. Volunteers help in activities ranging from engaging individuals in healthy activities to fundraising.

- Morrison Child and Family Services. Provides mental health, substance abuse and prevention services for children from birth through age 18.

- NAMI Multnomah. Serves people with mental illness and their families through support, education, and advocacy in Multnomah County. Volunteers teach, lead groups, and participate in events and fundraising.

- Serendipity Center. Helps at-risk children and their families; certified children's mental health provider. Volunteers help in classrooms in the garden and at special events.

- William Temple House. Provides immediate emergency social services and long-term solutions through mental health counseling and 1:1 dialogue case management services. Volunteers work in thrift store and food pantry and in dialog and case management.

- Volunteers of America Oregon. Finds innovative solutions to our community's most intractable social problems. Programs focus on children, family, public safety/substance abuse treatment, senior services.

Health-Based Support Organizations

The following is a list of health-based organizations – those that advance cures and treatment of a specific condition or disease. Programs may require background checks of volunteers. Visit their websites for more information.

- ALS Association of Oregon and SW Washington. Services and education for people with ALS, their families, caregivers, and healthcare professionals. Volunteers work in office, at outreach, educational and fundraising events.

- Alzheimer's Association. Participates in research, care and support and education to reduce risk of dementia through promotion of brain health.

- American Cancer Society. Dedicated to eliminating cancer as a major health problem through research, education, advocacy and service.

- American Diabetes Association: Dedicated to preventing and curing diabetes and to improve the lives of all people affected by diabetes.

- American Heart Association Portland. Dedicated to building healthier lives, free of cardiovascular diseases and stroke.

- Autism Research and Resources of Oregon. Autism research and services.

- Baby Blues Connection. Support, information and resources for women and families coping with pregnancy and postpartum mood disorders and professionals who serve them.

- Brain Injury Connections Northwest. Supports programs and services to improve the quality of life of those affected by brain injury.

- Camp Starlight. Camp. A week-long sleep-away summer camp for children whose lives are affected by HIV/AIDS.

- Candlelighters for Children with Cancer. Supports families affected by childhood cancer without regard to economics, race, religion, physician or healthcare facilities.

- Cascade AIDS Project. Works to prevent HIV infections; supports and empowers people living with or affected by HIV and eliminate HIV-related stigma and health disparities.

- Chelsea Hicks Foundation. A rolling dress-up closet that provides monthly dress-up parties for seriously ill children at Randall Children's Hospital and Doernbecher Children's Hospital. Tualatin.

- Children's Cancer Association. Provides a voice of experience, compassion and hope for families whose needs extend beyond medical treatment.

- Children's Healing Art Project. Teaching artists lead art adventures for children and their families at Doernbecher Children's Hospital, Knight Cancer Institute, the OHSU Pediatric Neurosurgery Clinic and Schnitzer Diabetes Health Center.

- Donate Life Northwest. Organ, eye and tissue donations to save lives.

- Easter Seals Oregon. Provides services to ensure that children and adults with autism and other disabilities or special needs and their families have equal opportunities to live, learn, work and play in their communities.

- HIV Day Center. Drop-in center for low-income people living with HIV/AIDS. Provides access to phones, a mail drop, computers, internet, WIFI, washer and dryer, clothing, shower and hygiene supplies, therapeutic and recreational activities.

- Katie's Kause for Cystic Fibrosis. Provides emotional support and temporary financial assistance to cystic fibrosis children and their families.
- Michelle's Love. Helps ease the stress of single parents undergoing cancer treatment by offering house cleaning, nutritious meals, transportation, and financial relief.
- Molly's Fund Fighting Lupus. Outreach and advocacy on behalf of those with lupus; partners with the medical community, doctors, hospitals and the insurance industry.
- MS Society of Portland. Working together to improve the quality of life for those with Multiple Sclerosis and their families.
- Muscular Dystrophy Association. Dedicated to finding treatments and cures for muscular dystrophy, amyotrophic lateral sclerosis (ALS) and other neuromuscular diseases.
- Northwest Down Syndrome Association. Creates and nurtures a loving and inclusive community celebrating every person with a disability including Down syndrome.
- Our House of Portland. Our House provides healthcare, housing, and other vital services to low-income people living with HIV.
- Parkinson's Resources of Southwest Oregon and Washington. Dedicated to improving the quality of life for people with Parkinson's Disease.
- United Cerebral Palsy of Oregon & SW Washington. Provides support for adults, children, and their families who experience cerebral palsy or other disabilities.

Hospice and End of Life Care

The following a list of hospice organizations. Programs may require background checks of volunteers. Visit their websites for more information.

- Adventist Health Hospice, Portland.
- Bloom Project. Provides fresh donated floral bouquets to hospice and palliative care patients weekly.
- Care Partners, Hillsboro.
- Comfort Hospice and Palliative Care, Portland SE.
- Community Home Hospice, Vancouver.
- Hospice Care of the Northwest, Portland NE.
- Housecall Providers. Portland SW.
- Kaiser Permanente Northwest Hospice, Portland.
- Legacy Hopewell House Hospice, Portland, SW.
- Legacy Hospice of McMinnville, McMinnville.

- Legacy Hospice Services, Portland SW.
- Mt. Hood Hospice, Sandy.
- No One Dies Alone. Volunteers compassionately hold a bedside vigil with patients in their last 24 or 36 hours of life. Jim Pfeifer 800-936-4756.
- PeaceHeath Hospice Southwest, Vancouver.
- Providence Hospice and Palliative Care, Several locations.
- Ray Hicky Hospice House, Vancouver.
- Seasons Hospice & Palliative Care, Portland.
- Serenity Palliative Care & Hospice, Tigard.
- Signature Hospice, Tigard.

Hospitals and Medical Centers

The following is a list of area hospitals and medical centers. Programs may require background checks of volunteers. Visit their websites or call for more information.

- Adventist Medical Center Portland, Portland.
- Doernbecher Children's Hospital, Portland.
- Kaiser Westside Medical Center, Hillsboro. 971-310-3135
- Kaiser Permanente Sunnyside Medical Center, Clackamas. 503-571-4155
- Legacy Emanuel Medical Center, Portland NE.
- Legacy Good Samaritan Medical Center, Portland NW.
- Legacy Meridian Park Medical Center, Tualatin.
- Legacy Mt. Hood Medical Center, Gresham.
- Legacy Salmon Creek Medical Center, Vancouver.
- Oregon Health & Science University, Portland, SW.
- PeaceHealth Southwest Medical Center, Vancouver.
- Portland Veterans Affairs Medical Center, Portland, SW.
- Providence Milwaukee Medical Center, Milwaukee.
- Providence Newburg Medical Center, Newburg.
- Providence Portland Medical Center, Portland NE.
- Providence Willamette Falls Medical Center, Oregon City.
- Shriners Hospital for Children, Portland.
- Tuality Healthcare, Hillsboro.
- Willamette Valley Medical Center, McMinnville.

APPENDIX J: HIKING AND WALKING RESOURCES

● Hikes Through Natural, Wildlife and Scenic Areas ● Outdoor Hike, Walk, Snow Sports Groups ● Community Education, Parks & Rec Programs ● Walk-Friendly Community Events ● Art and Cultural Meanderings

The following contains listings of area hiking and walking resources including a listing of hikes, by county, through natural areas, neighborhood walking resources, outdoor clubs and Meetup groups, community education programs, annual events and cultural diversions with a walking twist. More information is by visiting organization websites.

Hikes Through Natural, Wildlife and Scenic Areas

(Information courtesy of *Oregon Hikers Field Guide*)

Below are lists of hikes by county/city in the four-county region. You can find more detail at the Portland Hikes section of *Oregon Hikers Field Guide*, or section otherwise indicated. Boomers on the Loose™ obtained permission to publish a summary of the Guide's trail lists and descriptions for reference.

This Field Guide is an amazing resource for urban and wilderness hikers in Oregon and Southern Washington. Find a hike by location, difficulty (easy, moderate, difficult), by type (family hikes, backpackable snowshoe, off the beaten path), by environment (lakes, wildflowers, waterfalls, etc.) and several other categories. The Guide Describes trailhead locations, details about the hike, terrain, wildlife and points of interest along the way. It's written and updated by real hiker people! See for yourself.

The following list summarizes hike information from the *Oregon Hikers Field Guide*. Unless otherwise indicated, go to the *Portland Hikes* page in the on-line *Field Guide* for detail on hikes; scroll to your area of interest and select the hike.

Clackamas County, Clackamas/Milwaukee

- Elk Rock Island Hike, 1.3 miles. Rock hop Willamette River channel to ancient volcano.
- Mount Talbert Summit Loop Hike, 1.9 miles. Loop to summit of Mt. Talbert.
- Mount Talbert West Loop Hike, 1.9 miles. Forested loop.

- Mount Talbert from Sunnyside Road Hike, 2.6 miles. Climb Mt. Talbert from backside.

Clackamas County, Lake Oswego

- George Rogers Park Hike. 3.4 miles. Hike along and above the Willamette River. Lake Oswego.

- Springbrook-Iron Mountain Loop Hike. 34 miles. Two woodland parks; site of Prosser Iron Mine.

- Bryant Woods-Canal Acres Loop Hike, 1.7 miles. Natural areas near historic Oswego Canal.

- Luscher Farm-Cooks Butte Loop Hike. 4.4 miles. Variety of semi-rural public spaces on trails and streets.

Clackamas County, Mount Hood

- Mount Hood Area Hikes. More than 200 hikes of all lengths, difficulties, terrain, and scenery.

- Mt Hood Recreation Territory. Year-round recreation for all skill levels stretches from the mountain to rivers and lakes, our trails and other activities.

Clackamas County, Oregon City

- Clackamette Loop Hike. Loop in Oregon City and mouth of Clackamas River.

- McLoughlin Promenade Hike, 2.3 miles. Willamette Falls to McLoughlin House.

Canemah Bluff Loop Hike, 2.4 miles. Walk to clifftop viewpoints over Willamette and historic cemetery.

Clackamas County, West Linn

- Mary S. Young State Park Loop Hike, 3.7 miles. Native forest along Willamette River.

- Burnside Park-Maddax Woods Hike, 1.1 miles. Forest along Willamette River.

- Palomino Loop Hike, 1.9 miles. Narrow trails, down Trillium Creek, old growth trees, viewpoint.

- Wilderness Park Loop Hike, 2.2 miles. Two loop native forests connect the Camassia Natural area.

- Camassia Natural Area Loop Hike, 1.4 miles. Flower meadows.

- Fields Bridge Hike, 1.5 miles. Tualatin River walk. Glacial erratics, story of Willamette Meteorite.

Clark County

- Hikers and walkers can explore Vancouver's 15 parks and four trails many of which also are a haven for wildlife and migratory waterfowl.

- A 2.3-mile urban trail meanders through Fort Vancouver National Historic Site, Officer's Row, and Esther Short Park. Another urban trail connects downtown Vancouver to the picturesque Columbia River waterfront. A natural trail at the Whipple Creek Urban Wildlife Habitat allows hikers to view wildlife attracted by the habitat restoration.

Clark County, Battle Ground, Washougal, La Center

- Battle Ground Lake Loop Hike. 0.9 miles around Battle Ground Lake.

- Washougal River Greenway Loop Hike. 2.6 miles.

- La Center Bottoms Hike, 2.2 miles. Hike along East Fork Lewis River and extensive wetlands.

- Paradise Point Loop Hike, 1.8 miles. Swampy bottomland and forested slope hike on East Fork Lewis River.

Clark County, Camas, Washougal

- Lacamas Heritage Trail Hike, 7.0 miles. Flat hike along west sore of Lacamas Lake.

- Lacamas Creek Hike, 4.3 miles. Two waterfalls and a lake.

- Lacamas Park Lily Field Hike, 2.3 miles. Camas and fawn lilies in season.

- Round Lake Loop Hike, 1.5 miles. Walk around scenic lake.

- Washougal River Greenway Loop Hike, 2.6 miles. River using new footbridge

- Columbia River Dike Hike, 6.4 miles. Walk above the Columbia, views and wildlife.

- Steigerwald National Wildlife Refuge, 2.8 miles. Hike through 1,000-acre wetland, stand of Oregon white oaks, cottonwoods, and grassland.

Clark County, East Fork Lewis River

- East Fork Lewis River, several hikes totaling 27 miles. Battle Ground Lake, Lewisville Park Loop, Lucia Falls Loop, Moulton Falls, Yacolt Falls, Bells Mountain.

Clark County, Ridgefield

- Ridgefield National Wildlife Refuge. 5300-acre lush mixture of wetlands, grasslands, riparian corridors, and forests. Two of five habitat sections open to visitors.

Clark County, Rock Creek Area

- Three Corner Rock Hikes, several moderate to difficult hikes totaling 57 miles.

Clark County, Yacolt Burn

- Silver Star Mountain Hikes, several hikes totaling 40 miles.

Clark County, Vancouver

- Vancouver Discovery Loop Hike, 4.4 miles. Traces history of Anglo-American discovery and settlement.
- Waterfront Renaissance Trail, 5 miles. Views of I-5 and I-205 brides and Mount Hood.
- Burnt Bridge Creek Hike, 8.1 miles. Paved greenway in pretty valley.
- Ellen Davis Trail Hike, 5.2 miles. Up and around low hills in central Vancouver.
- Columbia Springs Hike, 3.1 miles. Network of trails east and west of Vancouver Fish Hatchery.
- Whipple Creek Loop Hike, 3.1 miles. Wind in and out of gullies in 300-acre forest.
- Kiwa Trail, 1.5 miles. Oaks to Wetlands Trail, 2 miles. Ridgefield National Wildlife Refuge.

Multnomah County, Gresham

- Gresham-Fairview Trail Hike, 6.7 miles. Paved trail passes backyards, industrial lots, creek, wetlands.
- Jenne Butte Hike, 3.3 miles. Forested cinder cone with two summits.
- Gresham Butte-Butler Creek Hike, 7.0 miles. Two Boring (city name) volcanoes, suburban greenway.
- Kelly Creek Loop Hike, 1.2 miles. Wetland and forest habit near restored suburban stream.
- Nakaka Loop Trail, 0.46 mile. Douglas Fir forest within Nadaka Natural area.
- Springwater Trail, 4.8 miles of asphalt multi-use path.

Multnomah County, Portland NE

- Kelley Point Loop Hike, 1.7 miles. Deciduous woodland and beaches, confluence of Willamette and Columbia Rivers.
- Smith and Bybee Lakes Hike, 2.1 miles. Urban wetland with large numbers of waterbirds.
- Hayden Bay Loop Hike, 2.5 miles. Paved path on Columbia River historic Lotus Isle Park.
- Whitaker Ponds Loop Hike, 0.5 miles. Quiet nature park on slough in industrial area.

- Rocky Butte Hike, 3.2 miles. Hike below cliff faces to park with expansive views.

Multnomah County, Portland NW

- Audubon Sanctuaries Loop Hike, 3.0 miles. Two short loops, optional diversion to Willamette Stone.

- Pittock Mansion Hike, 5.0 miles. Hike up to mansion expansive views of Portland and Mt. Hood.

- Hoyt Arboretum Loop Hike, 4.7 miles. Network of trails, view 1,100 species of trees.

- Washington Park Loop Hike, 3.9 miles. Hike to Arboretum, Portland Japanese Garden, Rose Garden.

- Council Crest Hike, 3.3 miles. Climb o summit with great views, minutes from downtown.

- Marquam Trail to Council Crest, 6.4 miles. Hike on section of 40 mile loop.

- Marquam Nature Park Loop Hike, 4.1 miles. Loop through Marquam Gulch, native forest.

- Forest Park, various trails. Dogwood-Wild Cherry, Maple-Wildwood, Firelane 7-Springville Road Loop, Tolinda-Ridge Trail Linnton Loop, BPA Road-Newton Road, Firelane 15.

Multnomah County, Portland SE

- Oaks Bottom Loop Hike, 2.3 miles. Hike part of Springwater Corridor. Water birds.

- Crystal Springs-Reed Canyon Hike, 2.4 miles. Botanical garden and small lake below gushing springs.

- Mt. Tabor Hike, 2.0 miles. Explore a volcano in town.

- Powell Butte, several trails totaling 11 miles. Mount Hood Trail Loop, Old Holgate, perimeter and summit hikes. Timber, meadows, dirt trails, paved path.

Multnomah County, Portland SW

- Woods Park Loop Hike, 2.1 miles. Native forest.

- Marshall Park Hike, 1.4 miles. Along Tryon Creek.

- Tryon Creek Loops, 7.6 miles. State park natural areas.

Multnomah County, Fairview/Troutdale

- Salish Ponds Hike, 2.8 miles. Restored ponds, forested Fairview Creek.

- Blue Lake Park Loop Hike, 2.0 miles. Park with natural area.

- Sundial Beach Loop Hike, 3.6 miles. Levee trail to beach at Sandy River.

- Oxbow Regional Park, three trails totaling 16 miles. Oxbow Loop, Alder Ridge Loop, North Oxbow Hike. Banks of Sandy River, buried forest, old growth woodland, ridge top, high bluff.

- Springwater Trail. Multi-use paved trail from Portland to Gresham. Connects several parks, wildlife, nature habitats.

Multnomah County, Sauvie Island

- Trails totaling 17 miles. Wapato Greenway Loop, Oak Island Loop, Warrior Point Hike.

Washington County, Beaverton

- Fanno Creek Beaverton, 8.5 miles. Suburban greenway, many trailheads.

- Commonweath Lake Loop Hike, 1.7 miles. Walk around suburban lake with winter waterfowl.

- Tualatin Hills Nature Park Loop, 4.3 miles. Many trails in mixed woodland.

Washington County, Forest Grove

- Hagg Lake Loop Hike, 13.5 miles. Forest, creek valleys and foothills reservoir.

Washington County, Hillsboro, Forest Grove

- Rock Creek Greenway Hike, 8.1 miles. Paved trail, hilly terrain along powerlines, past wetlands.

- Rock Creek-Orchard Park Hike, 5.0 miles. Paved trail along Rock Creek, wetlands and riparian vegetation.

- Noble Woods Loop Hike, 1.2 miles. Hike through lush woodland on Rock Creek.

- Rood Bridge Loop Hike, 2.6 miles. Short loops, confluence of Rock Creek and Tualatin River.

- Jackson Bottom Loop Hike, 2.9 miles. Borders Tualatin River. Education Center.

- Orenco Woods Loop Hike, 1+ miles in nature park, along Rock Creek.

- Fernwood Wetlands, 1.2 miles along main treatment pond, park and wetlands. Forest Grove.

Washington County, Tigard

- Fanno Creek Tigard Hike, 8.0 miles. Southern half of Fanno Creek greenway.

- Cook and Durham City Parks Hike, 5.7 miles. Natural areas along Tualatin River and Fanno Creek.

- Summerlake Park Loop Hike, 10 miles. Loop around suburban wetland.

- Cooper Mountain Loop Hike, 2.9 miles. Protects vanishing oak savannah in developing area.

Washington County, Tualatin/Sherwood

- Tualatin Refuge Nature Trail Hike, 2 miles. Along Tualatin River floodplain between Tigard and Sherwood. Birdwatching. Interpretative nature trail. Waterfowl.

- Chicken Creek Loop Hike, 2.8 miles. Late spring/summer access to riparian habitat in the Tualatin River Refuge.

- Browns Ferry Hike, 2.1 miles. Birdwatching walk on Tualatin River.

Outdoor Hike, Walk, Snow Sports Groups

The following contains listings of outdoor clubs and groups that sponsor Boomer-friendly outdoor activities. Visit their websites for more information.

- Bergfreunde Ski Club. Outdoor activities include hiking, snowshoeing and cross-country skiing.

- Cascade Prime Timers. Age 50+ actives who hike, ski, snowshoe, kayak, cycle and travel.

- Friends of the Columbia River Gorge. Nature advocates who sponsor hikes.

- Mazamas. A mountaineering education club that sponsors walks, hikes, mountaineering, ski, snowshoe and other outdoor sports events.

- Oregon Nordic Club. Promotes cross-country skiing.

- Oregon Sierra Club. Environmental advocates; also sponsors hikes.

- Oregon Walks. Sponsors neighborhood walks; promotes walking and making conditions for walking safe, convenient and attractive.

- Oregon Wild. Advocate for Oregon wildlands; also sponsors hikes, ski, snowshoe events.

- Portland Walking Tours. Offers specialty themed walking tours of unique places around Portland.

- Positively Portland. Walking tours that explore the architecture, history and culture of the Portland area.

- Racewalkers Northwest. Practices the racewalking technique for fitness and competition.

- Running Clubs. Running clubs that invite walkers to share their running routes: Clark County Running Club, Oregon Road Runners Club.

- Ten Toe Express. Free guided walks held from May through September, sponsored by City of Portland.

- Trails Club of Oregon. Year-round outdoor activities include hiking and snow sports.

- Volkssport Clubs. Area clubs organize free 5K and 10K non-competitive walks in scenic and historic areas and sponsor Year Round Walks, self-guided walks around the area. Columbia River Volkssport Club; Rose City Roamers, Portland SE; Cedar Miles Volkssport Club, Beaverton; Vancouver USA Volkssporters; All Weather Walkers, Vancouver.

- Wonders of Walking. Sponsors walking programs, training, fitness walking, clubs, for all levels. Fee.

- Uniquely Portland. Walking tours, day trips in and around Portland. Fee.

Examples of walk and hike Meetups and that may appeal to boomers are:

- Beaverton Nature Walks

- Eastside Women's Fitness

- Multiple Outdoor Activities for Boomers (MOAB)

- Oregon City/Beavercreek Women's Hiking/Outdoors

- PNW Women's Outdoor Group, Hiking in the Pacific Northwest

- Portland Veggie Hikers

- PDX Metro Pack Walks (w/dogs)

- River West Village Senior Walks

- Rose City Wanderers

- Walking Oregon and SW Washington

- Walk with Friends Hillsboro

- Why Not Fitness

Meetups come, go and change. Find current meetup descriptions and schedules at Meetup.com. Search by city, then by interest such as fitness, exercise, walking, hiking, etc. Sign up and show up.

Community Education, Parks & Rec Programs

The following is a list of community college and parks and recreation programs that offer seasonal walk and hike activities. Visit their websites for more information.

- Clackamas Community College (clackamas.edu). Open Community Education. Seasonal outdoor activities including hiking. 62+ may qualify for senior discount.

- City of Portland (portlandoregon.gov/parks). Open Senior Recreation Catalog. Seasonal outdoor activities including hiking. All levels.

- City of Tigard (tigard-or.gov/community). Tigard Walks. All about walking in Tigard, including maps.
- Clark College (ecd.clark.edu). Open Community Education Catalog. Outdoor activities and Mature Learning Program.
- Hillsboro Parks & Recreation (hillsboro-oregon.gov). Open Activities Guide. Seasonal outdoor activities including walking and hiking.
- Lake Oswego Community Center (ci.oswego.or.us). Open Current Catalog. Sponsors hikes and rambles within 2 hours, fee.
- North Clackamas Parks & Rec (ncprd.com). Open Find a Park, trails by city.
- Portland Community College (pcc.edu/community). Community Education programs including winter sports, kayaking, stand up paddling, birding.
- Tualatin Hills Park & Recreation District (thprd.org). Open Activities Guide, look for Elsie Stuhr Center 50+ Nature hikes, trips and tours.
- Vancouver (WA) Parks & Recreation (cityofvancouver.us). Fifty and Better. 50+ Forever Young Hikers, hiking outings, hiking orientation. Open Parks & Trails search.

Walk-Friendly Community Events

The following is a list of area walk and walk-friendly events.

For current event lists see Events12.com/Portland or Running in the USA, Portland.

- Shamrock Run. Includes 5K walk. Portland. March.
- Walk MS: Portland. Walk for multiple sclerosis. April.
- Camellia Run. Includes 10K and 5K walk/run. Newburg. April.
- Greater Portland Heart & Stroke Walk. American Heart Association. May.
- Relay for Life, American Cancer Society. Team relay walks at various locations around Portland. May.
- Portland Rose Festival. Grand Floral Walk. June.
- Vancouver USA Marathon. Walker friendly full and half marathon. June.
- Bridge Pedal. Walk, run, or bike over route crossing bridges. August.
- Portland Brain Tumor Walk. August.
- Sunday Parkways. Walkers, runners, and cyclists share traffic-free routes. Free. May-September.
- Portland Marathon and Half Marathon. Walker friendly full or half marathon. October.

Art and Cultural Meanderings

Add a little cultural variety to your walk. Check out this list of regular walkable Arts and Cultural events. Visit their websites for more information.

- First Tuesday Art Walk. Downtown Hillsboro. Art galleries and Washington County Museum.
- First Thursday, Pearl District. Galleries stay open late.
- First Friday, Portland eastside galleries, boutiques, eateries promote the arts.
- Last Thursday on Alberta. Showcases art, music and food. NE Portland.
- Tualatin Artwalk. Self-guided tour, public art, natural and cultural history.
- Tigard Art Walk. Art in downtown Tigard. May.
- SE Art ARTWalk. Artist in SE Portland. March.
- Tulip Fest. 40 acres of tulips and daffodils. Woodburn. April-May.
- Mt. Tabor Art Walk. Portland SE. May.
- Pioneer Family Festival. Oregon City. May.
- Memorial Weekend in Wine Country. Willamette Valley.
- Lake Oswego Festival of the Arts. Outdoor exhibits, performances. June.
- Gresham Arts Festival. July.
- Tualatin ArtSplash. Art Show. July.
- Alberta Street Fair. Local artists and crafts. August.
- Art in the Pearl. Art Festival, fine art booths. NW Portland, August.
- Oregon City Festival of the Arts. August.
- Art in the Pearl. September.
- Chalk Art Festival and Annual Corn Roast. Downtown Forest Grove. September.
- Beaverton Arts Mix. Art Show. October.
- Wine Walk. Art and wine in Lake Oswego. October.
- Wild Arts Festival. Nature in Art. November.
- Wilsonville Festival of Arts. November.
- Christmas in the Garden. 400,000 holiday lights. Oregon Garden. Silverton. December-January.
- ZooLights. 1.5 million holiday lights. Oregon Zoo. December-January.

APPENDIX K: HOBBY IDEAS FOR YOU!

Nearly any leisure activity we pursue or are passionate about can be considered a hobby. If you need ideas, scroll through the list below in alpha order by heading to see what sparks your enthusiasm.

Animals

- Beekeeping
- Bird watching
- Dog sports
- Foster animal, or special needs animal
- Pet sitting
- Pigeon racing
- Polo
- Showing dogs
- Taking care of pet
- Volunteering at animal shelter or rescue; animal therapy

Antiques

- Studying antiques and antiquing
- Teaching, public speaking, mentoring
- Writing, books, articles, blogs

Arts and Crafts

- Calligraphy
- Cake decorating
- Candle making
- Card making
- Coloring
- Crocheting
- Cryptography
- Decorative pillows
- Digital arts
- Drawing
- Flower (pressing, arranging)
- Glassblowing
- Jewelry making
- Knife making
- Lace making
- Macramé
- Model building
- Mosaics (tables, chairs, trays)
- Needlework (knitting, crocheting, cross-stitching or embroidery)
- Origami
- Painting, sketching (on canvas; or paint on glass or wood, murals, on furniture)
- Pottery and ceramics
- Quilting
- Rug making (easy rug hooking, braided rugs, etc.)
- Scrapbooking
- Sculpting
- Sewing
- Stained glass
- Teaching
- Taxidermy
- Whittling
- Wood carving
- Woodworking

Astronomy

Aviation

Blacksmithing

Boating - sailing and boating

Church/Religious Activities

- Serving/Volunteering (missions, outreach)
- Teaching, public speaking, mentoring

- Writing books, articles, blogs

Collecting Indoor Items

- Action figures
- Antiques
- Antiquities
- Art, paintings, sculpture, photography
- Books
- Beer signs
- Beer steins
- Cards
- Coins, stamps
- Comic books
- Dolls
- Elements
- Historical memorabilia
- Glassware
- Movies and movie memorabilia
- Postcards
- Records/Vinyl
- Sports memorabilia
- Stamps
- Toys
- Video games
- Vintage cars, jewelry, toys, signs, wine

- Teaching, public speaking, mentoring
- Writing, books, articles, blogs

Collecting Outdoor Items

- Flower collecting and pressing
- Fossil hunting
- Insect collecting
- Metal detecting
- Mineral collecting
- Rock balancing

- Sea glass collecting
- Seashell collecting
- Stone collecting
- Teaching, public speaking, mentoring
- Writing books, articles, blogs

Cooking

Dancing

- Salsa, tap, ballroom, country, jazz, square dancing, contemporary

Do It Yourself

- Book restoration
- Car/Truck restoration

- Ceramics (sinks, tiles, tile backsplash, creative cement work)
- Clock and watch repair
- Home renovation
- Interior decorating
- Small appliance or mechanical repair
- Soap making
- Trash to treasure projects
- Upholstery
- Teaching, public speaking, mentoring
- Writing books, articles, blogs

eBay Selling

Electronics

- Amateur radio
- Computers
- Video games

- Teaching, public speaking, mentoring
- Writing books, articles, blogs

Fashion

Fishing and Hunting

- Casting
- Deep sea fishing
- Fly fishing
- Hunting

Food and Drink

- Beer Brewing
- Cake decorating
- Cooking
- Smoking
- Specialized cooking
- Wine making (grape growing, wine study, classes)
- Coffee roasting
- Home brewing
- Teaching, public speaking, mentoring
- Writing books, articles, blogs

Games, Puzzles

- Board games
- Card games
- Chess
- Gambling

- Mind puzzles, Sudoku, Jigsaw puzzles
- Gaming (tabletop games and role-playing games)
- Teams and tournaments

Gardening

- Container
- Specialties (roses or exotic plants)
- Indoor (houseplants, conservatory, greenhouse)
- Parks (botanical gardens, zoological gardens)
- Residential (roof, atrium, balcony, window box, patio)
- Water gardening (pools ponds, bogs)
- Teaching, public speaking, mentoring
- Writing books, articles, blogs

Genealogy

Geology

Guns and Gunsmithing

History

- Art and Culture

- Local
- National
- Military
- Natural
- Political
- Teaching, public speaking, mentoring
- World
- Writing books, articles, blogs
- Volunteering

Internet – Web surfing

Lapidary

- Leather crafting
- Lego building
- Locksmithing
- Machining
- Magic
- Metalworking
- Modeling, scale modeling

- Trains, boats, structures, cars, tanks, planes, ships, action figures

Movies

- Watching, collecting, reviewing

Music

- Composing songs
- Listening to music, classical, country, rock, international
- Musical instruments
- Volunteer: playing music for nursing, retirement homes
- Teaching, public speaking, mentoring
- Singing
- Writing books, articles, blogs

Nature

- Bird watching
- Bird feeding
- Environmental volunteering
- Flower pressing

Outdoor Recreation

- Archery
- Astrology
- Astronomy
- Camping, Backpacking
- Birding
- Bocce Ball
- Canoeing
- Climbing
- Cycling
- Disc golf
- Fishing
- Gardening
- Geocaching
- Geology
- Horseback riding
- Hiking
- Hunting
- Kayaking
- Mushroom hunting/ Mycology
- Orienteering
- Skiing (downhill, cross-country)
- Snowshoeing
- Wildlife Viewing (bird watching)
- Writing
- Volunteering
- Teaching, public speaking, mentoring
- Writing books, articles, blogs

Performing Arts

- Acting
- Baton twirling
- Behind-the-scenes
- Cabaret
- Cosplaying
- Dancing
- Drama
- Juggling
- Musical instrument
- Singing
- Stand-up comedy
- Story Telling
- Theater
- Teaching, public speaking, mentoring
- Volunteering

Photography

- Classes

- Nature, weddings, babies, children
- Teaching, public speaking, mentoring
- Volunteering for non-profit

Printing

- Screen printing
- Lithography
- 3D printing

Public speaking

Puppets and puppeteering

Puzzles

Reading

- Book clubs
- Books, e-books, magazines, comics, newspapers, internet.
- Collecting
- Foreign language
- History
- Library volunteering
- Literature
- Novels
- Poetry group
- Teaching

Sewing

Shopping

- Antiquing
- Couponing
- Flea markets, farmers markets, craft markets

Sports - Outdoor

- Adventure races
- Air sports
- Archery
- Auto racing
- Aviation
- BASE jumping
- Baseball
- Basketball
- Beach Volleyball
- Bodybuilding

- Climbing
- Cricket
- Cycling
- Equestrianism
- Fencing
- Field hockey
- Figure skating
- Fishing (fly fishing, deep sea, casting)
- Football
- Flying disc
- Golfing
- Handball
- Hiking
- Horseback riding
- Hunting
- Ice hockey, ice skating.
- Inline skating
- Judo
- Kart racing
- Kayaking

- Kite flying, kite surfing
- Knife throwing
- Lacrosse
- Laser tag

- Marksmanship/ shooting
- Motor sports
- Mountain biking
- Mountaineering
- Nordic skating
- Nordic skiing
- Orienteering
- Pickleball
- Polo
- Pool/Billiards
- Racquetball
- Radio-controlled car racing
- Rafting
- Rappelling
- Rock climbing
- Roller derby
- Roller skating
- Rugby (league football)
- Running (jogging, cross-country, track & field)
- Sand art
- Scouting
- Shooting sports
- Skateboarding
- Skiing
- Skimboarding
- Skydiving
- Snowboarding

- Snowshoeing

- Softball
- Speed skating
- Squash
- Surfing
- Swimming
- Table tennis
- Taekwondo
- Tai chi
- Tennis
- Tour skating
- Triathlon
- Ultimate Disc
- Urban exploration
- Volleyball

Sports – Indoor

- Badminton
- Billiards
- Bowling
- Boxing
- Chess
- Curling

- Dancing
- Darts
- Fencing
- Gymnastics
- Martial arts
- Slot car racing
- Table football
- Volleyball
- Weightlifting

Sports - Water

- Aqua lung
- Canoeing, kayaking

- Paddle boarding
- Power boating (racing)
- Rowing, sculling
- Sailing (racing)
- Scuba diving, snorkeling
- Swimming
- Water skiing

Technology

- Computer skills (programming, apps hardware, software)

- Short-wave radio

Travel

Treasure Hunting – metal detecting

Volunteering

Woodworking

Writing

- Books (hobby interests)
- Creative writing (memoirs, fiction, non-fiction)
- Handwriting analysis
- Journalism (articles for newspapers, magazines)
- Letter writing
- Poetry group
- Web site/blog regarding your hobby or interest
- Write and/or illustrate a children's book
- Teaching, public speaking, mentoring
- Writing music

Yoga

APPENDIX L: LEARNING LOCATIONS

• Adult, Senior Enrichment Programs • University Lectures and Forums Open to the Public • Libraries • Public Libraries by County • Community Colleges Continuing Education • Parks and Recreation Programs • Senior and Community Centers

The following are lists of learning locations where you can attend classes and lectures, and learn from others, including libraries and community education programs. Visit their websites for more information.

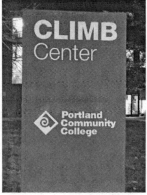

Adult, Senior Enrichment Programs

In addition to credit and non-credit community education classes, community colleges and some universities offer intellectual enrichment programs for seniors.

- Clackamas Community College Seasoned Adult Enrichment Program (clackamas.edu). educational experiences led by members, featuring talks by local speakers and authors, field trips and cultural activities. Or enroll in regular community education classes offered in Canby, Clackamas, Gladstone, Milwaukee, Oregon City and West Lynn. Seniors 62+ qualify for discounted tuition for many Community Education classes.

- Clark College, Mature Learning Afternoon Academics (clark.edu). Afternoon courses delve deeply into fascinating topics of history, science, religion or contemporary world problems. Enjoy the company of interesting people! Class fees apply. Clark does not discount tuition for seniors for regular classes.

- Portland Community College's Seniors Studies Institute (pcc.edu/resources). A program for dynamic older adults who want to expand their horizons and connect with others. Members plan, conduct and run the institute's programs and classes.

- Portland Community College (pcc.edu/community). Community Education programs in Multnomah and Washington Counties offer language and cultural classes, tours and volunteerism. PCC discounts senior tuition for community education classes.

- Portland Community College Life by Design (pcc.edu/climb/life). Provides discussion groups, workshops, classes and other resources for the -50 crowd. Salon: The Boomer Connection provides no-cost forums for meaningful discussion on a variety of topics.

- Portland State University, Senior Adult Learning Center. Oregon residents aged 65 and older may audit most of PSU's regular classes on a space-available basis and pay no tuition.

- Retired Associates of PSU (RAPSU). A group of retirees from PSU who organize and attend a variety community programs and lectures. Membership open to the public.

University Lectures and Forums Open to the Public

The following is a list of colleges and organizations that sponsor events such as student and facility lectures, classes, music and arts performances and other learning forums that are open to the public. Many are free. See their websites for more information.

- City Club of Portland (pdxcityclub.org). Friday Forums of local issues and topics welcome non-members.

- Literary Arts (literary-arts.org). Portland Arts & Lecture bring celebrated writers, artists and thinkers to the community.

- Marylhurst University (marylhurst.edu). Many cultural activities open to the community. See Calendar descriptions.

- Maitripa College (maitripa.org). Public programs, Buddhist and divinity studies.

- Oregon College of Oriental Medicine (ocom.edu). Sponsors various public events.

- Oregon College of Art and Craft (ocac.edu). Offers free lectures and collaborations.

- Oregon Health & Science University (ohsu.edu). Various lectures, events and programs open to the public.

- Oregon Humanities (oregonhumanities.org). Various humanities-related public events, conversations and collaborative projects.

- Pacific Northwest College of Art (pnca.edu).

- Washington State University, Vancouver. See Events Calendar, some lectures open to the public. See descriptions.

- Reed College. Various art exhibitions, concerts, lectures and other events open to public.

Libraries

The following contains listings of libraries and library systems where you can browse a schedule of classes, lectures, events and historical talks. See *Public Libraries by County* below a list of libraries by county.

- Beaverton City Library. Author lectures, cultural, historical talks and classes.

- Clackamas County Libraries. Author lectures, musical and other programs.
- Clark County Libraries. Fort Vancouver Regional Library. Events and discussion groups.
- Hillsboro Libraries. Regular programs. Search calendar for events by keyword, location, event types, and age group.
- Multnomah County Libraries. Regular lectures and author talks. Search for library events and classes by location, audience, type of event, dates, etc.
- Washington County Libraries. Regular programs. Search calendar for events by keyword, location, event types, and age group.

Public Libraries by County

The following is a list of libraries in and around Portland listed by county, many of which are supported by Friends of groups.

Clackamas County

The members of the Library District of Clackamas County share a single computer system so individuals can borrow materials from any library in the system. Local city or county libraries tailor collections and programs to the unique needs of patrons.

- Canby Public Library. Free resources, helpful staff, and educational programs for all ages. Volunteers: Shelve books and materials, process new and pick lists, deliver books to homebound; help special events and projects.

- Estacada Public Library. Explore the present, the past and the future through all forms of communication. Features art created by members of the community.

- Gladstone Public Library. Books, resources and programs for Gladstone residents. Volunteers: Help with shelving, holds and shelf reading. Seeks volunteers with Spanish and technology skills.

- Happy Valley Library. Houses over 100,000 items for all ages, including books, audio books, DVDs, CDs, magazines, kits, E-Books, E-Audio books and computers. Friends of the Happy Valley Library.

- Lake Oswego Public Library. Provides publishing, programs, classes, community resources, gathering place. Volunteers: clerical work, data entry, fund-raising. Book drop pickup, Booktique delivery, cart revising, genealogical services, shelf reading.

- Ledding Library of Milwaukie. Volunteers (adult section) shelve library materials, repair books, telephone people with overdue items and shelf read. Children's Library volunteers help prepare for craft projects and do shelving and shelf reading.

- Molalla Public Library. Provides a wide range of library and information technology resources and programs. Friends of the Molalla Public Library.

- Oregon City Public Library. Volunteers: shelve/shelf reading, special projects, magazine processing, clean DVDs, assist with summer reading and craft programs. Friends of Oregon City Public Library.

- Clackamas County Library. Oak Grove. Friends of the Clackamas County Library.

- West Linn Public Library. Volunteers: Shelve library materials, keep shelves organized, and participate in occasional special projects.

- Wilsonville Public Library: Book, media and art collections, bookstore, computer and WiFi, cultural passes, home delivery, notary, conference room, test proctoring. Volunteers: adults to seniors, assist in bookstore, cleaning, home delivery, shelf reading, shelving, special computer projects. Friends of the Wilsonville Public Library.

Clark County

Fort Vancouver Regional Library District. Regional library district with multiple libraries; all citizens have access to professional information services staff, internet access, world-class research databases, and a collection of more than 730,000 books, magazines, DVDs, audiobook CDs, and audiobook and video PlayAways®, downloadable and streaming music, videos, eBooks and audiobooks.

District libraries include:

- Battle Ground
- Cascade Park
- District Headquarters
- Goldendale
- La Center
- North Bonneville
- Ridgefield
- Stevenson
- The Mall
- Three Creeks
- Vancouver
- Washougal

- White Salmon Valley
- Woodland
- Yacolt
- Yale

Multnomah County

Multnomah County Library System. The largest library system in Oregon is comprised of multiple branches offering books, magazines, DVDs and computers, including nearly 900 public computer stations and a collection of two million books and other library materials. Libraries in the system include:

- Albina Library. Portland NE
- Belmont Library. Portland SE
- Capital Hill Library. Portland SW
- Central Library. Portland SW
- Fairview-Columbia Library. Portland NE
- Gregory Heights Library. Portland NE
- Gresham Library. Gresham NW
- Hillsdale Library. Portland SW
- Holgate Library. Portland SE
- Hollywood Library. Portland NE
- Kenton Library. Portland NE
- Library Administration. Portland NE
- Midland Library. Portland SE
- North Portland Library. Portland NE
- Northwest Library. Portland NW
- Rockwood Library. Portland SE
- Sellwood-Moreland Library. Portland SE
- St. Johns Library. Portland NE
- Title Wave Used Bookstore. Portland NE
- Troutdale Library. Troutdale
- Woodstock Library. Portland SE

Washington County

Cooperative Library Services – Washington County libraries share materials to provide excellent county-wide library service to all residents.

- Banks Public Library

- Beaverton City Library. Volunteer. New Friends of the Beaverton City Library.

- Beaverton City Library @ Murray Scholls.

- Cedar Mill Community Library. Volunteers: Library page (shelving, holds processing, "tasket" processing.) Resale shop, technical services, instructor, computer technology. Beaverton.

- Cedar Mill Community Library @ Bethany. Volunteers: Library page (shelving, holds processor, "tasket" processor.) Resale shop, technical services, instructor, computer technology.

- Cornelius Public Library Cornelius. Volunteers: Assist in circulation, computers, children's programs, processing, mending and other special projects.

- Forest Grove City Library Forest Grove. Volunteers: Sort and check-in books, search for hold items; shelve books; shelf-reading, data entry, special events.

- Garden Home Community Library

- Hillsboro Brookwood Library. Volunteers: Shelve books, process new library items, help at book sales, special events and programs; provide individual computer, technology, homework help.

- Hillsboro Shute Park Branch. Volunteers: Shelve books, process new library items, help at book sales, special events and programs; provide individual computer, technology, homework help.

- Oregon College of Art & Craft.

- North Plains Public Library.

- Sherwood Public Library. Volunteers: Help behind the scenes to make materials ready for check-out.

- Tigard Public Library. Volunteers: Fill requests, shelve, sort books, tasket support, A/V verification.

- Tualatin Public Tualatin Library. Volunteers: Check in and shelve items, process and repair books, CDs and other materials; repair materials.

- West Slope Community Library. Friends of the Library.

Other Libraries

- Genealogical Forum of Oregon, Inc. Genealogy services. Library Volunteers work as reading room research assistants. Other Volunteers work in book cataloging, book sales, data entry, data extracts, manuscripts, print shop; research assistants.

- Tuality Healthcare Library

Community Colleges Continuing Education

Community colleges offer credit and non-credit community education classes on a wide spectrum of learning interests. Find out more in seasonal catalogs available on-line or in print.

- Clackamas Community College (clackamas.edu). Open Community Ed catalog. 62+ may qualify for senior discount.
- Clark College (ecd.clark.edu).
- Mt. Hood Community College (mhcc.edu). Senior discounts.
- Portland Community College (pcc.edu/community).

Parks and Recreation Programs

Check the quarterly activities calendars of area parks and recreation programs for adult and senior group classes and activities such as creative arts, crafts, music, dance, bird watching, outdoor activities, games, history and much more.

- Hillsboro Parks & Recreation (hillsboro-oregon.gov). Open activities guide, includes Senior Activities.
- North Clackamas Parks and Recreation District (ncprd.com). Open Discovery Guide.
- Oregon City Parks & Recreation (orcity.org/parksandrecreation). Classes through Pioneer Senior Center.
- Portland Parks & Recreation, (portlandoregon.gov/parks) Open Senior Recreation Catalog.
- Tualatin Hills Park & Recreation District (thprd.org). See Activities Guide.
- Vancouver Parks & Recreation (cityofvancouver.us/parksrec). Catalog Activity Guide. 50 and Better Activities.
- Wilsonville Parks & Recreation (wilsonvilleparksandrec.com). Open Activity Guide. Active Adults program.

Senior and Community Centers

Senior and adult community centers offer classes, programs and other learning opportunities on a wide variety of topics such as health education, technology, arts, music, local history and much more. See *APPENDIX P, Community and Senior Centers* on page 182 to find one near you.

APPENDIX M: MUSEUMS, HISTORICAL SITES, SOCIETIES

The following is a list of museums and historical sites in the Portland area. For more information about the organization, special events, programs and lectures, as well as volunteer opportunities, visit the organization's website.

- Architectural Heritage Center/Bosco-Milligan Foundation. Preserves historic character and livability of buildings, places and neighborhoods to promote reuse of period homes and buildings through programs, tours and exhibits.

- Blue Sky Gallery. Oregon Center for the Photographic Arts. An exhibition and explication space, community research center, and archive for contemporary photography in Portland.

- Canby Historical Society Depot Museum. Railway and local history museum at Oregon's oldest train station.

- Clackamas County Historical Society and Museum of the Oregon Territory. Early history of Clackamas County and research library.

- Clark County Historical Museum. Exhibitions and programs that explore Clark County's past, present and future.

- Crown Point Vista House. Stone building with views of Columbia River Gorge features displays on history and geology of the Gorge.

- Design Museum Portland. A nomadic museum of all things design focused on educating the world about design. A distributed museum with exhibits and events all over town. Events, field trips, exhibits, story tellers, film screenings.

- Fort Vancouver. A place to explore the lands and structures at the center of fur trade and military history in the Pacific Northwest of the area's diverse cultures. Walking trails. Volunteer at Fort Vancouver, the McLoughlin House and Pearson Air Museum.

- Friends of Lone Fir Cemetery. Community volunteers strive to preserve the headstones of the deceased, the greenspace they exist in and the stories of its residents for future generations.

- East County Historical Organization. Preserve the history of the Fairview, Rockwood and Wilkes areas of East Multnomah County, Oregon.

- Evergreen Aviation and Space Museum. Large display of military and civilian aircraft and spacecraft; home of original Spruce Goose.

- Genealogical Forum of Oregon. Genealogical library. Genealogy classes.

- Gresham Historical Museum. Educates the public on Gresham's cultural history, including the people and events that make Gresham the city it is today.

- Historic Belmont Firehouse. A display of artifacts owned by Portland Fire and Rescue. 900 SE 35th Avenue, Portland. 503-823-3615.

- Horace Baker Log Cabin. Pioneer Church and stagecoach. Carver, OR.

- Interactive Museum of Gaming and Puzzlery. One of the largest publicly accessible collections in the world. Thousands of games, puzzles and related materials from many countries and traditions.

- Interpretive Center at the End of the Oregon Trail. Preserves our heritage, educates the public and interprets the history of the Oregon Territory, Clackamas County and Oregon City, the western terminus of the Oregon Trail.

- Kidd Museum. Houses the lifetime collection of Frank Kidd. Includes displays of primitive toys. Portland. (503) 233-7807.

- Milwaukee History Museum. Museum of the Milwaukee Historical Society.

- Molalla Museum Complex. Historical structures, farm equipment and history; emphasis on Native Americans early pioneers, timber industry.

- Movie Madness Video. A museum of movie memorabilia including 100 pieces of costumes and props from silent era to classics.

- Museum of Contemporary Craft. Located at Pacific Northwest College of Art, a vibrant center for investigation and dialogue that expands the definition and exploration of craft.

- Northwest Museum of Rocks and Minerals. Houses a world-class collection of fine rocks and minerals, fossils, meteorites, lapidary art, and gemstones from the Pacific Northwest and around the world. Volunteer.

- Old Aurora Colony Historical Museum. Preserves the history of the heritage of the Aurora Colony. Aurora.

- Oregon Electric Railway Museum. Restores and operates old electric railway cars, equipment, trams, streetcars and trolleys. Displayed at Antique Powerland in Brooks.

- Oregon Historical Society Museum. Preserves, collects and publishes Oregon's multicultural history through museum exhibitions, research collections and publications.

- Oregon Jewish Museum and Center for Holocaust Education. Archives of the Jewish Historical Society of Oregon.

- Oregon Maritime Museum. The Museum's steam sternwheeler Portland is moored at the Willamette River in downtown Portland's Waterfront Park.

- Oregon Military Museum. Official military history repository; military arms and ordnance, military vehicles, aircraft, equipment. Clackamas.

- Oregon Museum of Science and Industry. Science and technology museum and a leading science center.

- Oregon Nikkei Legacy Center. Shares and preserves Japanese American history and culture in Portland's Old Town neighborhood, where Japantown once thrived. Volunteer.

- Oregon Rail Heritage Foundation. Preserves and displays Portland's historic locomotives, railroad equipment and artifacts; educates public about Oregon's rich and diverse railroad history.

- Pittock Mansion Society Historical Mansion. Turn of the century structure available for tours and rentals.

- Portland Art Museum. Engages and enrich diverse communities through the presentation, interpretation, and conservation of art and film.

- Portland Children's Museum. Youth programs in art, nature and theater. Exhibits, parties, trips, classes, teaching and learning.

- Portland Chinatown History and Museum Foundation. Honors, preserves, and interprets history and cultural heritage of the area's Chinatowns.

- Portland Police Museum. The Portland Police Museum features permanent and rotating exhibits. Police memorabilia, equipment, photos.

- Portland Puppet Museum. Museum of puppets, place for puppet shows.

- The Hat Museum. Private collection of hats to see and for sale.

- Troutdale Historical Society. Maintains three museums, the Harlow House farmhouse, the Depot Rail Museum and a Barn Exhibit Hall.

- Washington County Museum. Discover the unique culture and history of the Tualatin Valley.

- Wells Fargo History Museum. Learn how Wells Fargo connected Oregon communities by stagecoach and steamboats on the Columbia and Willamette Rivers.

- World Forestry Center. Educates and informs people about the world's forests and trees, and environmental sustainability.

APPENDIX N: ON THE WATER RESOURCES

• Outfitters That Offer Classes and Guided Trips • Community Classes and Tours • Kayak Clubs, Rowing Clubs, Meetups

The following list contains listings of various organizations and clubs that

provide equipment, lessons, tours and adventures for paddlers of all ages and abilities. Visit their websites for more information.

Outfitters That Offer Classes and Guided Trips

The following are outfitters who offer classes and guided group tours as described on their websites.

- Alder Creek. Downtown Portland. Sponsors the annual Spring Paddle Festival.
- eNRG Kayaking, Oregon City
- Next Adventure. Portland SW
- Portland Kayak Company. Portland SW
- Ridgefield Kayak Rentals
- Scappoose Bay Paddling Center

Community Classes and Tours

Several organizations provide classes and tours to beginner as well as experienced paddlers. Check their activities guides and websites for current schedules and information.

- Hillsboro Senior Center Activities. Activities Guide. Spring kayak classes.
- Lower Columbia Estuary Partnership. Summer canoe paddles in 12-person canoes.
- Motivated Zen. Puts paddlers in unique and beautiful environments. Portland.
- North Clackamas County Parks & Recreation. Adult Outdoor Programs, kayak touring class.
- Portland Community College. Kayak tours in natural areas.
- Tualatin River Keepers. Guided paddle trips May through October. Led by trained volunteer trip leaders, each trip has a different focus. Beginner to advanced paddlers. Gear provided.
- Willamette River Riverkeepers. Discovery river paddle (kayak or canoe) trips from Eugene to Portland.

Kayak Clubs, Rowing Clubs, Meetups

The following is a list of outdoor and kayaking clubs and Meetups that include paddling sports adventures and classes. Visit their websites for more information.

- Bridge City Paddling Club. Competitive dragon boat and outrigger canoe club.

- Cascade Prime Timers. Outdoor club with canoe/kayak activities.

- Bergfreunde Ski Club. Ski and outdoor club with kayak activities.

- Golden Dragons. Senior, 50 and older group of active men and women dragon boaters.

- Kayak Portland. Diverse group, welcomes all skill levels.

- Oregon Kayak & Canoe Club. Organizes river trips at all skill levels, while strengthening the boater community. Education, tours, social activities.

- Kayak Heroes. Whitewater kayakers.

- Oregon Ocean Paddling Society. Explores lakes, rivers, bays and oceans of the Pacific Northwest. Education, tours, social activities.

- Oregon Whitewater Association. All river users including kayakers, canoeists.

- Pacific NW LGBT Kayaking Club. Lesbian and gay kayak enthusiasts who enjoy exploring the waters of Oregon, Washington, and Pacific Ocean. Open to all.

- Portland Kayak & Canoe Team. Adult and youth kayakers and canoeists who seek to become more skillful, fit, or competitive.

- Portland Sea Kayakers. Information website for sea kayakers. Year-round schedule of whitewater and flat/moving water trips for canoeists and kayakers.

- Tualatin River Paddlers. Kayak, canoe, or SUP, for families and individuals, all levels.

- Willamette Kayak and Canoe Club. Organizes trips on all types of water, all over Oregon western states. Training.

- Wasabi Paddling Club. Dragon boat paddling teams, workouts, all levels. Welcomes new paddlers.

- Portland Kayaking Community. For first-timers as well as seasoned kayakers.

- Vancouver Lake Dragon Boating. Dragon boating, kayaks, rowing. All skill levels.

APPENDIX O: TEACH-TALK-TUTOR-TRAIN PLACES

• Schools, Universities and Colleges • Libraries and Museums • Senior and Community Centers • Medical Centers • Parks and Recreation Programs • Community Service Tutoring

The following contains listings of various organizations that you can contact for opportunities to share your knowledge and expertise.

The contact process will vary by type of organization so start by visiting the organization's website, viewing a catalog of courses, visiting the volunteer web page or contacting the organization directly by phone or email to ask for the appropriate contact person.

Schools, Universities and Colleges

In addition to credit and non-credit community education classes, community colleges in all four counties offer teaching and speaking opportunities and generally provide contact information in their course catalogs. Interested speakers may also contact the college directly.

- Clackamas Community College Seasoned Adult Enrichment Program (clackamas.edu). Provides educational experiences led by members, featuring talks by local speakers and authors, field trips and cultural activities. Community Education programs offered in Canby, Clackamas, Gladstone, Milwaukee, Oregon City and West Lynn.

- Clark College, Mature Learning Afternoon Academics (clark.edu). Afternoon courses delve deeply into fascinating topics of history, science, religion or contemporary world problems. Enjoy the company of interesting people!

- Mt. Hood Community College Community Education. (mhcc.edu/ce). Class offerings in fitness, language, crafts, health, music, gardening, business and finance, computer skills and more.

- Portland Community College's Senior Studies Institute (pcc.edu/resources). A program for dynamic older adults who want to expand their horizons and connect with others. Members are speakers and plan, conduct and run the institute's programs and classes.

- Portland Community College (pcc.edu/community). Community Education programs in Multnomah and Washington Counties offer language and cultural classes, tours and volunteerism and welcome applications for teaching classes.

- Portland Community College Life by Design (pcc.edu/climb/life). Provides discussion groups, workshops, classes and other resources for the after-50 crowd taught by guest speakers. Salon: The Boomer Connection provides no-cost forums for meaningful discussion on a variety of topics.

Libraries and Museums

Libraries and museums offer programs and teaching opportunities on a wide variety of topics. Library programs tend to focus on author programs, teaching technical skills and language; museums offer history learning. Libraries also offer how-to programs on all varieties of hobbies, arts & crafts and writing and publishing. Because the contact process varies by organization, start by contacting the individual library or museum directly.

See *APPENDIX L, Public Libraries by County* on page 163 and *APPENDIX M: MUSEUMS, HISTORICAL SITES, SOCIETIES* on page 167 for lists.

Senior and Community Centers

Senior and adult community centers offer programs on a wide variety of topics. Interested speakers should contact the center directly and ask for the person in charge of events and programs. See *APPENDIX P, Community and Senior Centers* on page 182 to find one near you.

Medical Centers

Most healthcare organizations in and around Portland offer health-related classes and events to their members and to the community at large. Some have online classes and videos.

Ongoing, popular classes are healthy eating, fitness and exercise, weight management, smoking cessation, healthy lifestyles, support groups, reducing stress, pain management, depression, yoga and many other health topics related to seniors and retirees. Classes are listed on websites and selected from the website classes page.

Interested speakers should contact an organization directly and ask for the person in charge of classes and events.

- Adventist Health (adventisthealth.org) select Classes and Events.
- Kaiser Permanente (kp.org)
- Legacy Health (legacyhealth.org)
- Providence Health (oregon.providence.org)
- Tuality Healthcare (tuality.org/tuality)

Parks and Recreation Programs

The following is a list of area parks and recreation organizations. People interested in teaching should start by viewing the organization's activity catalog, visiting the organization's website for contact information. Or contact the organization directly asking for the person in charge of classes and events, or the human resources or employment department.

- Hillsboro Parks & Recreation (hillsboro-oregon.gov). Open activities guide, includes Senior Activities.

- North Clackamas Parks and Recreation District (ncprd.com). Open Discovery Guide.

- Oregon City Parks & Recreation (orcity.org/parksandrecreation). Classes through Pioneer Senior Center.

- Portland Parks & Recreation, (portlandoregon.gov/parks). Open Senior Recreation Catalog.

- Tualatin Hills Park & Recreation District (thprd.org). Open Activities Guide.

- Vancouver Parks & Recreation (cityofvancouver.us/parksrec). Catalog, see 50 and Better Activities.

- Wilsonville Parks & Recreation (wilsonvilleparksandrec.com/). Open Activity Guide. Active Adults 55+ Programs & Services program.

Community Service Tutoring

Following are examples of schools and non-profits that seek tutors to help children with reading, art, music and sports, as well as social skills. Opportunities and requirements are generally posted on an organization's volunteer page. Background checks may be required.

- AC (Active Children) Active Children Portland keeps children active through sports, creative writing, nutrition education, and service learning projects. Volunteers sell raffle tickets at sports events; are assistant coaches and writing/service learning mentors, and work at special events.

- Aperture Project. Engages young people through photography and creative writing, giving them the opportunity to express themselves in new ways, exploring their everyday lives and that of other young people.

- Caldera Caldera. A catalyst for transformation of underserved youth through year-round art and environmental programs. Volunteers provide administrative and special events support and direct services to youth.

- Camp Fire Columbia. Partners with local kids, schools, families; offer programs that support academic achievement, build social and life skills, foster community engagement, and develop career, college readiness. Volunteers help with fundraising, work at youth camp, food pantries, help youth with career paths.

- Children's Healing Art Project. CHAP teaching artists lead art adventures for children and their families at Doernbecher Children's Hospital, Knight Cancer Institute, the OHSU Pediatric Neurosurgery Clinic and Schnitzer Diabetes Health Center.

- Financial Beginnings. Works in partnership with schools, community organizations and other nonprofits to deliver age appropriate financial education. Volunteers present financial programs in schools grades 4-12.

- Focus on Youth. Provides mentoring and hands on learning experiences for disadvantaged and homeless youth. Offers Seeds of Hope, a youth leadership program incorporating science, math, photography and gardening for homeless youth. Volunteers help students build and plant gardens, teach photography and take youth on photography field trips.

- Girls Inc. of the Pacific Northwest. Inspires girls, ages 6-18, to be strong, smart, and bold. Our gender-specific programs designed to provide girls with the confidence and self-esteem for a bright and economically-independent future. Volunteers are media and STEM professionals, mentors, guest speakers and trip hosts.

- Growing Gardens. Volunteers build organic vegetable gardens at homes, schools and correctional facilities. Supports low-income residents with resources and education to grow their own food. Volunteers build garden beds, lead teams, work with home gardener, present workshops, nutrition education, youth clubs, classroom assistants. Portland NE.

- HOBY Oregon - Hugh O'Brian Youth Leadership. Provides youth selected by their schools opportunities to participate in unique leadership training, service-learning and motivation-building experiences.

- I Have A Dream Foundation Oregon. Addresses problem of low graduation rates among disadvantaged and low-income youth by adopting a low-income school serving highest poverty neighborhood elementary school. Volunteers mentor young Dreamers and host field trips at businesses.

- Metropolitan Family Service. Supports community school programs, mentors children, delivers holiday gifts to disabled and older adults, provides transportation, works at fundraising. Americorps National Service Network, AARP Experience Corps.

- Metropolitan Youth Symphony. Provides music for underserved schools and low-income youth learning an instrument for the first time.

- Minds Matter of Portland. Transforms the lives of accomplished high school students from low-income families by broadening their dreams and preparing them for college success. Volunteers mentor students.

- OHDC YouthSource. Assists youth to obtain educational credentials while receiving support services; high school credit courses, employment training and job development services in SE Washington County.

- OSU 4-H Youth Development Program. Helps young people learn and grow in partnership with caring adults to develop the skills and confidence needed to become contributing, productive, self-directed members of society. 4-H uses an active, learn-by-doing approach.

- Outside In. Helps homeless youth and others move toward improved health, self-sufficiency. Services include housing, education, employment, counseling, medical care, healthy means, recreation and safety.

- p:ear. Builds positive relationships with homeless and transitional youth ages 15-24 through education, art and recreation to affirm personal worth and create more meaningful and healthier lives.

- Portland OIC / Opportunities Industrialization Center. Reconnects alienated at-risk youth affected by poverty, family instability and homelessness; with high school education and with career training. Mentor and supports our graduates in post-secondary education.

- Portland YouthBuilders. Supports young people who are committed to changing their lives to become self-sufficient, contributing members of the workforce and their community. Volunteers tutor and speak to classes about their career, conduct mock interviews, host students at workplace.

- Rock 'n' Roll Camp for Girls. Builds girls' self-esteem through music creation and performance. Provides workshops, technical training; creates leadership opportunities, cultivates supportive peer and mentor community; encourages social change and the development of life skills.

- Sauvie Island Center. Educates kids about food, farming and the land. Volunteers lead small preschool groups through high school-aged students through interactive, hands-on, farm-based lessons.

- SMART Program (Metro Area). Adult volunteers help children learn to read. Volunteers are paired with children for reading sessions.

- STAGES Performing Arts Youth Academy. Offers performing arts classes and workshops for children and young adults Volunteers design and construct costumes and serve on the board and various committees.

- The Dougy Center. Provides support in a safe place where children, teens, young adults, and families grieving a death can share their experiences. Volunteers facilitate groups, help in office, do yard and building maintenance, fundraising, marketing and speaking and training.

- The Portland Kitchen. A no-fee, comprehensive year-long after-school culinary program to low-income and at-risk youth ages 14-18. Provides no-cost four-day-per-week summer program.

- Vibe of Portland. Offers affordable visual-arts and music classes to low-income neighborhoods through in-school, afterschool and studio classes and camps. Volunteers teach classes, help at workshops, put on shows.

- Youth Progress Association. Provides youth with the living skills, structure and support needed to transition successfully into the community. Serves highest risk youth.

APPENDIX P: VOLUNTEERING RESOURCES

● Senior-Specific Volunteer Organizations and Resources ● Pay It Forward: Serving Older Adults ● Community and Senior Centers ● Volunteer Websites and Organizations

The following contains listings of volunteer opportunities specifically for older adults and seniors and for organizations that provide services to seniors which welcome senior volunteers. Also listed are organizations that match volunteers to multiple community needs.

Senior-Specific Volunteer Organizations and Resources

The following is a list of senior volunteer organizations that specifically seek the wisdom and experience of retirees and seniors for their programs. Visit their websites for more information.

- AARP Experience Corps. A national program (local at Metropolitan Family Service) which taps experience and passion of adults age 50 and over to ensure that every child has a chance to succeed in school and in life. Volunteers are academic tutors and mentors, work one-to-one and in small groups to help kids K-3 develop literacy skills and self-confidence.

- Clackamas County Retired and Senior Volunteer Program. Refers and places skill and experience of seniors in non-profit and public organizations in education, arts, science environment and culture. Commitments range from annual events to seasonal projects to ongoing weekly schedules.

- Elders in Action. Advocates for older adults, provides meaningful volunteer opportunities and works to build an age-friendly community. Personal advocate, age friendly businesses. Volunteers perform outreach at resource fairs, wellness events, farmers markets and civic gatherings. Presentations to civic groups and businesses.

- Jesuit Volunteer EnCorps. Recruits and supports volunteers 50 and older in part-time, meaningful service positions where they have a direct impact on people living in the margins.

- Retired and Senior Volunteer Program. Provides opportunities for retired people age 55 and older to volunteer in their community, including helping with senior assistance activities. Volunteer. Vancouver.

- SAGE (Senior Advocates for Generational Equity). Inspires people over 50 to give of their time, talent and passion to enable younger and future generations to thrive. Volunteers host socials, work as ambassadors, speak and help on a variety of initiatives.

- SCORE Portland. Counselors to America's Small Business. Provides free business mentoring services to entrepreneurs. Volunteers provide confidential mentoring services, lead seminars and workshops, expand outreach of through marketing and alliances in local communities. Subject matter expertise by industry and professional skills.

- SCORE Vancouver. Counselors to America's Small Business. Provides free business mentoring services to entrepreneurs. Volunteers provide confidential mentoring services, lead seminars and workshops, expand outreach of through marketing and alliances in local communities. Subject matter expertise by industry and professional skills.

- Senior Corps/Oregon. Connects today's over 55s with the people and organizations that need them. Volunteers are mentors, coaches or companions to people in need, or contribute their job skills and expertise to community projects and organizations. Portland.

- VIEWS: Volunteers Involved in the Emotional Wellbeing of Seniors. Promotes emotional well-being of seniors through peer counseling and social engagement. Volunteers facilitate discussion groups to provide emotional support, unconditional listening and sharing of experiences.

Pay It Forward: Serving Older Adults

The following is a list of non-profits and other organizations that serve older adults and depend primarily on volunteers, including those who want to pay it forward. Visit their websites for more information.

- AARP Real Possibilities. Helps seniors search for local volunteer opportunities. Search by keywords and zip code.

- AARP Tax-Aide Program. Volunteers assist seniors preparing tax returns. Supported and operated by CASH Oregon. Portland.

- Clackamas County Senior Services. Programs range from transportation to in-home care for seniors and their families. Works with community partners to advocate on behalf of older adults at state and federal level. Volunteers assist seniors and others in need of services.

- Clark County Volunteer Connections. Connects the wisdom, experience and talents of volunteers with community volunteer opportunities. Volunteers serve at hospitals, schools, nursing homes, and agencies that serve seniors and others in need.

- Elders in Action. Advocates for older adults, provides meaningful volunteer opportunities and works to build an age-friendly community. Personal advocate, age-friendly businesses. Volunteers perform outreach at resource fairs, wellness events, farmers markets and civic gatherings. Presentations to civic groups and businesses.

- Institute on Aging, Portland State University. Institute faculty, staff and students are dedicated to enhancing understanding of aging and facilitating opportunities for elders, families, and communities to thrive.

- Meals on Wheels People/Loaves & Fishes Centers. Assist seniors in maintaining independence by making nutritious food, social contacts and other resources easily accessible at dining centers or delivered. Volunteers delivery meals, work in dining rooms and at special events.

- Metropolitan Family Service. Supports community school programs, mentors children, delivers holiday gifts to disabled and older adults, provides transportation, works at fundraising. AARP Experience Corps.

- Multnomah County Aging, Disability and Veterans Services. Serves older adults (age 60 and older), people with disabilities age 18 and older, and veterans. Helps individuals identify resources to enable and promote independence, dignity and choice. Volunteers serve on Elders in Action Commission advisory group and Multicultural Action Committee.

- Project Linkage. Metropolitan Family Service program that serves older adults and people with disabilities who need in-home support or transportation services to remain independent in their homes. Volunteers provides transportation to/from grocery stores, medical appointments and other places.

- Ride Connection. Provides transportation for older adults and people with disabilities, as well as transportation solutions for the community at large. Volunteers are drivers, ride ambassadors, help in office, on committees, with advocacy and advisory councils.

- Retired and Senior Volunteer Program. Provides opportunities for retired people age 55 and older to volunteer in their community, including helping with senior assistance activities. Volunteer. Vancouver.

- Community and Senior Centers. Located in communities throughout our area, senior centers provide a range of social services to help seniors live, learn, thrive, and socialize. Senior Centers also offer a variety of services including legal aid counseling, health education programs and activities, e.g. dancing, tai chi, yoga. Senior centers rely on volunteers in a variety of roles.
  - Teach classes in fitness, arts and crafts, writing.
  - Maintain libraries.
  - Cook and serve meals.
  - Assist with technology and computers.
  - Lead trips.

See a list of Community and Senior Centers on page 182 to find one near you.

- Store-to-Door. Volunteers deliver groceries from store to seniors and people with disabilities.

- Urban League of Portland Senior Services Program. African American culturally specific programs for seniors aged 60 and older. Connects seniors with services that allow them to remain safely in their homes. Volunteers are fundraisers, designers, accountants, web developers, board members and mentors; office work and events.

- Villages Northwest. An all-volunteer group of people working together to create options for people to age and thrive in their homes. Village groups in area communities include both retired and working people. Volunteers provide services such as transportation, social visits and light household tasks, as well as outreach, administrative and office tasks. Volunteers work in all phases of start-up and ongoing operations of providing services.

  These villages are in various stages of development or operation:

  o Eastside Village PDX. Portland, East.
  o Village Without Walls. Hillsboro-Forest Grove area.
  o Three Rivers Village. Clackamas County.
  o Viva Village. Beaverton.
  o North Star Village, North Portland.
  o NE Village PDX. Portland, Northeast.
  o River West Village. SW Portland. In development.
  o Villages Clark County. Includes all of Clark County, Washington: Vancouver, Camas, Washougal, Battle Ground, and others.

- Volunteers of America Oregon-Senior Programs. Programs dedicated to helping seniors and adults with disabilities remain as healthy and independent for as long as possible. Programs serve seniors, adults with disabilities, those with special needs such as with Alzheimer's or other dementias, post-stroke, Parkinson's and other diagnoses. Volunteer, one-time projects. Volunteer, ongoing positions.

- Washington County Disability, Aging, and Veteran Service. Provides programs and services to maintain and enhance the quality of life to assure that basic needs are met for Washington County seniors, veterans and people with disabilities. Volunteers serve on advisory council, advise seniors on health insurance, work on REACH program, work in senior centers, provide Gatekeeper training, help clients enroll for benefits, and lead living well workshops.

- Write Around Portland. Writing workshops for seniors and low-income individuals. Free creative writing workshops in hospitals, shelters, senior centers, prisons, schools and treatment facilities. Volunteers help produce books, set up book readings and parties, help with outreach and mailings, provide childcare, facilitate or assist in workshops.

- YWCA of Greater Portland Services Program. Offers support services to low-income seniors that allow them to maintain healthy and independent lives in the safety and comfort of their own homes.

Community and Senior Centers

The following is a list of community adult and senior centers by county. Visit their websites for more information about classes, programs, fitness activities, day trips, social groups, volunteering and other services and activities.

Clackamas County

- Canby Senior Center, Canby

- Estacada Senior Center, Estacada

- Gladstone Senior Center, Gladstone

- Hoodland Senior Center, Welches

- Lake Oswego Adult Community Center, Lake Oswego

- Milwaukie Senior Center, Milwaukee

- Molalla Senior Center, Molalla

- Pioneer Community Center, Oregon City

- Sandy Center, Sandy

- Sherwood Family YMCA

- West Linn Adult Community Center

- Wilsonville Community Center

Clark County

- Battle Ground Senior Center, Battle Ground, WA

- Clark County YMCA, Vancouver WA

- Luepke Senior Center, Vancouver, WA

- Washougal Senior Center, Washougal, WA

Multnomah County

- Charles Jordan Community Center, Portland, N

- East Portland Community Center, Portland, SE

- Friendly House Senior Center, Portland, NW

- Gresham Senior Center, Gresham

- Hollywood Senior Center, Portland, NE

- Ikoi-No-Kai, Portland, NE

- NE Community Center Portland, NE

- Neighborhood House Elm Ct Center, Portland, SW
- Neighborhood House Senior Center, Portland, SW
- Portland Impact Multi-Cultural Senior Center, Portland, SE
- Rose Center for Seniors, Salvation Army, Portland, NE
- Urban League of Portland, Portland, NE

Washington County

- Beaverton Hoop YMCA
- Community Senior Center, Hillsboro
- Elsie Stuhr Center, Beaverton
- Forest Grove Senior & Community Center
- Marjorie Stewart Community/Senior Center, Sherwood
- North Plains Senior Center
- Tigard Senior Center
- Tualatin Juanita Pohl Center

Volunteer Websites and Organizations

The following is a list of volunteer websites that connect volunteers to multiple opportunities within their communities and organizations. Visit their websites for more information.

- AARP Real Possibilities. Helps seniors search for local volunteer opportunities. Search by keywords and zip code.
- Clackamas County Retired and Senior Volunteer Program. Refers and places skill and experience of seniors in non-profit and public organizations in education, arts, science environment and culture. Commitments range from annual events to seasonal projects to ongoing weekly schedules.
- Clackamas County Volunteer Connection. Connects individuals to volunteer service with over 200 community organizations including Senior Centers, food pantries, youth and family programs, homeless programs and other community support programs.
- Clark County Volunteer Connections. Connects the wisdom, experience and talents of volunteers with community volunteer opportunities. Volunteers serve at hospitals, schools, nursing homes, and agencies that serve seniors and others in need.
- Cornelius, City of. Volunteer opportunities with various community services and Boards and Commissions such as Budget Committee, Parks Advisory Committee, Library Board, Planning Commission and Community Oriented Policing Citizen Advisory Board.

- Forest Grove Volunteers. Links to volunteer needs in government, on Boards and Commission, Library, Fire and Rescue, Parks, Police Reserve, Senior Center and Adelante Mujeres.

- Hands on Greater Portland. Connects volunteers with more than 300 nonprofit agencies in the metro area that need volunteers. Build a house. Done-in-a-day or longer in-depth opportunities.

- Hillsboro, City of, Oregon Volunteers. Links to volunteer information in various city departments such as Emergency Response Teams, Parks & Rec, Police, Public Library, Boards and Commissions.

- Gresham, City of. Volunteer program including Boards and Committees, community building activities and natural resources and public safety programs.

- Lake Oswego, City of. Volunteer opportunities. Links to descriptions of various departments such as adult community centers, Boards and Commissions, Public Works, Gardens, Library, Parks & Rec, Farmers Markets and more.

- Milwaukee, City of. Volunteer opportunities on various Boards and Commissions and in various community facilities, services and events.

- Multnomah County Citizen Volunteer Bank. Links and descriptions of volunteer opportunities in different county boards and committees such as the Citizen Involvement Committee or Citizen Budget Advisory Committees, as well as other opportunities throughout the county.

- Portland Community College. Volunteer Opportunities Newsletter. Publishes newsletter of community organizations with volunteer opportunities.

- Portland Parks & Recreation. Offers a variety of volunteer opportunities at sites across the city. Volunteer coaches, teacher aides and mentors always needed in youth programs – and the parks, gardens, and natural areas welcome extra hands. Ongoing and one-day projects.

- Tigard, City of. Volunteer opportunities on Boards and Committees such as Budget, Transportation, Pedestrian and Bicyclist, Neighborhood Involvement and others.

- Troutdale, City of. Volunteer opportunities on various committees such as Budget, Citizens Advisory, Parks, Planning and Public Safety.

- Tualatin, City of. Volunteer opportunities on various advisory boards and committees and in various community services including the library.

- SOLVE Oregon. Mobilizes over 35,000 volunteers serving over 1,000 cleanup and restoration projects throughout the state. "We clean, restore, educate and involve our community through volunteerism."

- United Way. Connects individuals, families, groups, and workplaces to volunteer opportunities. Hundreds of nonprofits list ways to get involved weekly; groups or individuals.

- Vancouver, City of. Volunteer programs. Opportunities in work parties and in departments, on Boards and Commissions, Fire, Neighborhood Associations, Parks, Police, Recreation, Water Resources.

- VolunteerMatch. Volunteer website that helps volunteers get in touch with nonprofits, government agencies and causes that need them.

- Volunteers of America Oregon. Provides a range of services to the area's most vulnerable populations. Volunteers help thousands of families in the greater Portland, Oregon and Vancouver, Washington areas. Volunteer, one-time projects. Volunteer, ongoing positions.

- Washington County Volunteers. Links to volunteer information in various county departments: Boards & Commissioners, Clean Water, District Attorney, Emergency Management, Health & Human Services, Land Use & Transportation and Sheriff's Office.

- Wilsonville, City of. Links to Board and Commission positions, library volunteers, parks maintenance, and community services such as senior companions, transportation and other community services.

ACKNOWLEDGEMENTS

Thank you (I think) to the many people who didn't try to dissuade me from an enormous and often daunting research and publishing journey to create Boomers on the Loose™ in Portland.

My painfully honest and patient editor, Bill Cowles, a long-time friend and colleague, infused a light-hearted tone and spirit into the content to make a lot of information friendly and accessible. Graphic designer Lyn Birmingham helped create the wide-eyed cover personality, using illustrator and cartoon artist Josh Cleland's (Portland's) "the West Side" poster artwork (JoshCleland.com). Josh's drawing perfectly captures the countless directions and options retirees choose from in Greater Portland.

Thanks to Jackie B. Peterson, author and business advisor for the Portland Community College SBDC program, for her enthusiastic encouragement and advice. Others in the PCC Life by Design program offered numerous referrals to resources and contacts.

Thanks to many other friends, colleagues and contacts for support and advice including many hiking buddies and area non-profits, outdoor clubs, meetups, writing and other organizations.

Photo Acknowledgements

9, 75	Bonnie Hayes Animal Shelter
12	Popcorn Clouds children's books, NW Book Festival
13	Rogue Bluegrass Band at outdoor market
14	Summer outdoor concert, Cathedral Park
15	Encore Senior Players performers
15	Storyteller, Art of the Story Festival
21	Trails Club of Oregon work party
23	Jackson Bottoms Wetlands environmental education
24	Lunch with Birds program, Hillsboro Parks & Recreation
27	Mobile Kitchen sponsored by St. Vincent DePaul
29	Group bike ride, Trails Club of Oregon
30	Seattle to Portland cycling event
32, 42 (top)	Group hike with AARP, PCC Life by Design
33	Pickleball with Age Celebration, Hillsboro
35-38	Rogerson Clematis Collection and Garden, volunteers, and community garden at Luscher Farm
37	Learning Garden at Jenkins Estate
39, 107, 109, 110, 119	Sidewalk drawings, Valley Art Association Chalk Art Festival
41, 125	Group hike, Milwaukie, Oregon
42, 61	Walk with Friends Meetup, Hillsboro, group social hikes
43	Outdoor sculptures, University of Portland campus
65, 67	Village Without Walls volunteers. Photo on page 67 by Lyn Birmingham
68	Sherwood Senior Center music entertainer volunteer
117	Children's Book Bank volunteers, Wordstock book festival
124	Sunday Parkways summer cycling

INDEX

ABOUT THE AUTHOR

Janet Farr (Jan) is a self-proclaimed authentic Boomer on the loose. Typical of Baby Boomers reaching that "certain age," Jan seeks to re-invent her 40+ year career experience as a business and technical writer. She also shares that boomer-typical desire to pursue meaning in her next phase in ways that make a positive difference in the lives of others.

Jan is a transplant from the Kansas City area, and before that, central Michigan. In 2009 she finally took steps to realize her dream to experience the Pacific Northwest outdoor lifestyle and culture unique to Portland.

Jan enjoys the many threads of Portland's rich fabric – hiking, walking, snowshoeing, traipsing through cities and burbs. Exploring the forests, wetlands, mountains, gardens, the coast, wine country, the gorge, downtown and more. Experiencing the quirky arts and culture scene – thriving side-by-

side with the high-profile – the caring-for-people attitude, the amazing summers and yes, even the rain making the elegant ruggedness possible.

Not to mention, abundant beginner photo opportunities.

She's cursed with an eagerness to research and organize vast amounts of information into useful chunks that delight, surprise and help her Boomer audience.

And what better subjects than hundreds of leisure ideas, options and opportunities just waiting for reinventing Boomers, and what better place than in and around Portland.

CPSIA information can be obtained
at www.ICGtesting.com
Printed in the USA
FSOW02n2244290717
36774FS